BASIC IDEAS and STRATEGIES to Help Parents and Educators Raise Successful Children with Inner Discipline

*I saw an angel in the stone and
I carved to set it free.*

DOUG WHITENER

PAGE PUBLISHING, INC.
New York, NY

First originally published by Page Publishing, Inc. 2019

ISBN 978-1-68456-288-6 (Paperback)
ISBN 978-1-68456-289-3 (Digital)

Printed in the United States of America

I saw an angel in the stone and I carved to set it free.

—Michelangelo

Acknowledgements

This book is dedicated to the small group of cancer patients who bravely participated in the first clinical trials of the new melanoma biologic drugs that are beginning to revolutionize cancer treatments. Only 25% of you survived the next few years, but *all* of you have contributed to the development of better cancer treatments in our lifetimes. This book could not have been written without your sacrifices.

I wish to especially thank my wife, Rosa, and our sons, Gary and Ray, for their support in the development of this book. My stories are your stories, and it has been quite a ride full of fun and adventure punctuated by love.

I have been blessed in my career to have been surrounded by teachers and educational staff who are some of the best people on this earth. Your dedication to students has inspired me to write this book, and you have conspired to make me a better person in so many different ways.

Special thanks to Dr. David Minor of the San Francisco Oncology Associates and his medical staff along with the nurses at California Pacific Hospital in San Francisco for the enduring care you gave me leading to a second chance at life. The staff and students of Peavine Elementary School in Reno, led by Kathy Achurra and Mary Rivara, joined my immediate family, sisters Jean, Julia and Gale and friends to provide a powerful community of support during my darkest days.

I am very fortunate to have been mentored by some truly remarkable people in my lifetime. I cannot reference all of your names, but I would like to mention a few individuals who have had a very positive influence on my life and the ideas presented in this book: Bill, Beverlee and Jim Whitener, Jerry Crawford, Anneli Crawford, John Mikesell, Ron Beck, Rick Harris and my walking partners, Neil Schott and Terry Fowler.

Introduction

A. My calling

In the fall of 2004 I was enjoying my job as the principal of Peavine Elementary School in Reno, Nevada, when a medical event changed my life dramatically. The melanoma cancer cells that attacked me unexpectedly five years earlier had returned with a vengeance. I was in trouble. I had transformed from a comfortable school principal in the sunset of his career to a fifty-three-year-old adult fighting for his life with a stage 4 cancer diagnosis. Sometimes I wonder if the young medical student who stumbled to announce the return of my melanoma on a rainy afternoon could have ever understood the impact of the four words he shared with me that day and the new path my life was about to take.

Cancer has been my curse, but it has also been my blessing. Fourteen years later I have survived chemotherapy, interleukin therapy, remission, relapse, experimental drug trials, and difficult side-effect events. In 2018, I am alive, I am well, and I am a changed person. I have come to appreciate the small miracles that we encounter minute to minute, hour to hour and day to day in our homes, community and living on our earth. Gratitude and appreciation have become important parameters of my life. The child playing on the beach no longer represents a toddler running on the sand; instead, this child has become the embodiment of natural imagination, discovery, and boundless energy all harnessed in one small package of innocence. Equally important, I am taking the time to pause and appreciate the bliss this little child has in his life and the joy child-hood can give to my life if I allow myself to be a present witness.

Just as I have happily learned to appreciate the small wonders of life, I have also learned to respect the realities of the "short visit" we have on this earth. I often remind myself of a quote by Mahatma Gandhi that I try to recite frequently:

> Live as if you were to die tomorrow.
> Learn as if you were to live forever.

Strangely enough, this wonderful quotation by Gandhi is as much challenging as it is freeing. In a most forceful way, Gandhi reminds us that neither illness nor age should ever prevent us from making our best effort to take advantage of every minute we have on this earth and to learn more about ourselves *and* the community of earth we live in. My good friend Carl Meibergen once pointed out that the real challenge of silver maturity is not that we stop learning; rather, we face the reality that we will ultimately run out of time to complete our learning. I share Carl's perspective, and it causes me to want to sprint, not coast home. Hence, my book has been written to enhance my journey through life and, hopefully, to celebrate my learning in a way that may be helpful to others attempting to find their parenting or teaching voice.

It is important for me to point out that I do not consider myself an *expert* when it comes to child development or school discipline. I am just a man who, working together with my wife, managed to be a part of a loving parent team for two wonderful young men. We handled some issues well as parents and struggled with other issues. I have had a forty-five-year career in education highlighted by success with most students and my share of failures. The credentials I have to write this book are borne from the rich and diverse experiences I have had, my interest in reading the ideas of others and my willingness to reflect upon my experiences to develop new and better ideas. Judge me as you would judge a baseball manager who was not a great player but has succeeded to use the wisdom of his reflections from his past to guide his team to victory. Confucius addressed this element of wisdom best when he said:

> By three methods we learn wisdom: first, by reflection which is the noblest; second, by imitation, which is easiest; and third by experience, which is the bitterest.

B. My voice

> Find your voice and help others to find their voice.
>
> —Stephen Covey, 2004

A good starting point in one's endeavor to learn about and understand ourselves better is to *find our voice* (Covey, 2004). I must say that my undertaking to write this book represents a journey to find my voice and to express it in a manner that might be helpful to others. Just as an athlete strengthens his health by *running*, I believe that finding my voice and *writing* about it strengthens my understanding of who I am.

What is my voice and how do I find it? I believe a person's voice is revealed by examining how passionate the person is about actions in his/her life. In my forty-five years as an educator, I have been a parent, teacher, coach, counselor, school psychologist, special education administrator, university instructor, and a principal. A theme that has crossed over all these fields has been my interest in helping students improve their behavior in responsible ways. Call this discipline or call it counseling; it is a "calling" of mine that has always been readily apparent to my colleagues and, now, to myself. Combine this passion for helping students improve themselves with a deep appreciation of the miracles of child development, and you have a glimpse into what I consider to be *my voice.*

C. Pause and reflect

> How much more precious is a little humanity
> than all the rules in the world.
>
> —Jean Piaget

We all have a voice, but few of us in life have near-death experiences that cause us to appreciate our voice so much and recognize that the creation of our legacy is *time-stamped*. I would not have written this book if I had not had a cancer "wake-up call" and understood that it was time to explore and celebrate my voice and share it with others.

When I prepared for my lunchroom duty on a Friday in November of 2004, I realized that this would probably be the last time I would ever work in a school. I was scheduled to begin a six-month course of intermittent chemotherapy requiring hospitalization the next Monday. I knew that stage four malignant melanoma was almost always fatal within seven months of diagnosis. Not only would I probably not return to school, I would not be on this earth when school started the next fall. The fifty-minute duty I had that day was one of the most meaningful events in my life. Let me explain.

I had always enjoyed visiting with the students at lunchtime, but today was different. It was a spiritual experience for me because I keenly recognized how privileged I had been as a principal and teacher to daily witness the fun, imagination, loving, and challenging experiences of children finding their way in a sometimes confusing world. I was consumed by gratitude and by sorrow at the same time as I walked down the aisles talking to students and opening milk cartons, possibly for the last time.

I remember my tour through the third-grade tables and bestowing upon each student a magical power. "Today you are Spiderman," I announced to one student who I knew had a hard life and struggled in school. The little guy beamed at me, stood up, flexed his arm triumphantly, and announced to his classmates that he was going to save the world. This was not a new game for me and the kids; it just had more meaning today. At this point in time I was "pausing" to celebrate the imagination and resilience of this young boy who had found his voice for one single moment sitting with two hundred other students in the Peavine Elementary School multipurpose room. This child's enthusiasm and imagination quickly allowed me to ignore my sorrow and to celebrate my status as a witness and contributor to the miraculous unfolding of child imagination.

The inescapable truth about this moment was that you don't have to have cancer to appreciate the wonders of children and to recognize what a special profession educators find themselves in. The cancer experience, however, does create a "pause" in life when one can choose to review the meaning of his/her life experiences and become more appreciative of daily life happenings. At the end of most chapters in this book I have included a "Pause and Reflect" section that is intended to cause the reader to think about and celebrate the experiences we are privileged to have as educators and parents.

I sometimes stumble when I am asked whether this book is written for parents or educators. The obvious answer to this question is that this book is written for both audiences, but the reasoning behind this concept is a bit more complex. Parents are each child's first teacher, and teachers are "in locus parentis" for children in their classrooms. That is to say, teachers legally and ethically assume many parenting responsibilities in the classroom, and effective parents are unquestionably teachers in their home. The same principles of child development are in play at home as well in the classroom. If a boy pushes his sister at home, the parent faces the same dilemma as the teacher who must contend with a boy pushing a girl out of the way in the classroom. Effective responses to these situations by mindful parents and teachers who understand basic principles of child guidance are a key focus of this book.

It is no coincidence that when I am asked to address a group of educators about behavior guidance, I request that I be allowed to address parents in the evening. It is my belief that parent participation, collaboration and alignment with school learning and behavior practices are key factors found in successful schools.

D. My beliefs

The starting point for any good discussion of behavior guidance is, of course, the *beliefs* that form the foundation for good guidance systems. The child guidance practices that are expressions of my beliefs will be discussed extensively in the book, but my beliefs are properly discussed in this Introduction.

I think it is critical that the adults working with children take the time to dialogue about the core beliefs they have regarding childhood behavior. Developing a consensus description of *shared* beliefs can be the first step in developing a parents' or educators' *mission statement*. Borrowing a term from the construction industry, the mission statement can be seen as the blueprint for supporting the child as she or he develops into an adult.

I was surprised when I came to see that my eight major beliefs fit nicely together to form the acronym CORE TEAM. Inherent in this acronym is the concept that the adults in children's lives must work together as a team and identify core beliefs that guide their actions. My beliefs are listed below and they will be discussed in more depth in the book. It is not coincidence that the first two beliefs cited are the most important beliefs:

- Childhood is to be *celebrated*.
- Child misbehavior needs to be seen by teachers and parents as an *opportunity for learning*. The goal of this learning is to help children develop the inner discipline they will need to be successful in life.
- *Relationships* trump substance; the children I have had the most success with have been the children who trusted me and knew I cared about them. Adults who make the extra effort to have empathy for students have a greater chance for success when working with these students.
- There are no easy formulas for raising children. Parents and teachers must be willing to *experiment* with interventions designed to help children be successful in their ventures.

- Teaching, practicing, monitoring, and reinforcing developmentally appropriate behavior works better than punishing negative behavior to create lasting adaptive behavior. Childhood discipline is a *teaching process*
- *Each child* has his strengths and a unique spirit to be appreciated. It is our job as the adults visiting the child's world to help the child to learn and develop his/her gifts, manage his weaknesses and help the child to find his voice
- *Aligning* teacher, school, and family practices creates the greatest chances for school success. The chances for student success are increased geometrically when parents and teachers collaborate to help the child learn and grow as a person
- The behavior teachers and parents *model is* just as important as what they teach. It is important that educators take the time to reflect upon their own behavior to see if it is consistent with their beliefs

E. Academic acknowledgments

I am, foremost, a practitioner in the world of education. I am keenly aware, however, that I have been influenced by the ideas of several great thinkers in the fields of education, psychology, and leadership. I would like to briefly share some of the major ideas of these theorists that have influenced me in my life and in my career:

- I have read and reread Stephen Covey's books, the *Seven Habits of Effective Leaders* (1989) and *The Eighth Habit* (2004), because these books have had so much meaning to me. You will see quotes from Dr. Covey sprinkled throughout this book. Whether we realize it or not, parents, and teachers are leaders in every sense of the word, and Dr. Covey presents some great ideas regarding principled leadership.
- The theories of Abraham Maslow have had a major influence upon me. Whenever I cannot determine the purpose

of a child's behavior, I find myself searching for "unmet needs" that are driving the student's misbehavior.

- What modern theorist could totally reject the ideas of B. F. Skinner and his behavioristic learning theory? I have come to accept the power of learning theory, but I reject the tendency to become too enthralled with learning theory to the point of sacrificing the important human qualities that separate us from other animals. The social learning theories of Albert Bandura have been easier for me to accept than the stringent learning theories of B. F. Skinner.

- I do believe that we must pay attention to the thinking of children and their perspective on events. As such, one could say I am very influenced by the cognitive theories of Karen Horney and Albert Ellis. I strongly believe that our belief system heavily influences our emotions and our actions.

- Finally, during my term as an interim principal at the High Desert Montessori School in Reno, Nevada, and as a board member of the school I have learned to appreciate the ideas of Maria Montessori. I try to remember a quote from her whenever I am involved in a disciplinary action with a child (Montessori, 1967):

> Too often a teacher commands because he is strong and expects a child to obey because he is weak. Instead of acting in this way, an adult should show himself to a child as a loving and enlightened guide assisting him along the way leading to the kingdom of heaven.

F. Book organization

This book has been divided into eleven chapters:

1. Strengthening Wings: Love and Appreciation

The first seven chapters of this book have focused primarily upon basic parenting and teaching behaviors that help children to strengthen their wings as they prepare to fly into their future. Interestingly enough, the emphasis in these first seven chapters is as much on the parents and teachers trying to guide the child as it is on the child.

In the first five chapters many adult behaviors at home and in classrooms that tend to bring out the best in children are reviewed. This section of the book, of course, begins with the concept that children are to be appreciated, and we must all take the time to "witness" the joys of childhood. Unconditional love, paying attention to emotional growth, creating optimal learning environments, and helping children to find and successfully pursue their individual strengths are concepts that are discussed.

In chapter 6 the parents and teachers reading this book are asked to look inside themselves to find clues that may help explain their first impulses when they respond to child behavior. One can never underplay the importance of our family backgrounds as an influence upon our behavior. Learning to understand and appreciate the influence of our background and striving to not let our past experiences control our responses to children becomes the ultimate challenge of an *inside-out approach* to parenting and teaching. The chapter ends with an emphasis on the importance of adults caring for themselves so they are better prepared to take care of their children.

All successful sculptors have a purpose for their creations. Some do their carvings to sell them inexpensively at a craft fair, some carve to celebrate the beauty of life and others carve to make others think about life's deepest mysteries. There must be a purpose for their artwork that guides their actions and creations. The same type of purposeful thinking must guide parents and teachers as they embark on their journey to support the healthy development of children. The focus of chapter 7 is upon the need for parents and teachers to develop a *mission statement* that guides their actions and influences the decisions they make for and with the children they serve.

In chapter 8 the focus of the book changes course from the fundamentals of raising children to the *fundamentals of child discipline*. This change in course makes sense when one broadens the definition of discipline to include all the steps teachers and parents make to guide the behavior of children. Let us never forget that when a parent or teacher chooses a strategy to respond to a child's behavior, his or her values, mission, relationship with the child, and beliefs are put into play. Child discipline becomes the vehicle for translating the family and school mission statements into actions that help each child to develop his or her inner discipline. Throughout this chapter one theme constantly reappears: *discipline interactions always present a teaching opportunity.* A considerable amount of time is spent on exploring the teaching component of disciplinary actions taken by adults who are determined to help children grow from their misbehavior adventures.

When a child misbehaves, the beliefs of the adults responding to the misbehavior must be translated into *discipline strategies.* In chapter 9 specific discipline strategies are discussed in detail with an emphasis on careful listening, meaningful logical consequences, restorative justice, firm enforcement, and the very important follow-up discussion. In all situations the adults responding to childhood misbehavior are cautioned to focus upon the event that has occurred and not the character of the child. Equally important, the goal to help each child develop *inner discipline* must always be on the mind of the adult who is intervening to help the child learn from his or her behavior.

In chapter 10 the flow of the book changes from preventing major discipline problems to responding to major discipline patterns. Understanding the *purpose of misbehavior* becomes a major topic in this discussion. The concept of a PTR (prevent, teach, and reinforce) is introduced as a tool to assist parents and teachers who are struggling to help children change their course of behavior. The importance of teamwork, proactive planning, consistency, and persistence is highlighted in this chapter.

Chapter 11 was written to address the needs of children who require, at certain times in their life, extra help to be successful in our society. The author refers to these children as *intensive-care children* because of their need for enhanced support and services. There is a level of optimism in this chapter because of the author's belief that children who need extra care in their lives can grow to become their own caregivers later in life. The challenge that parents and teachers face is to recognize when a child is in need of special help, and to provide that help in a timely and effective manner. The chapter concludes with the stories of two extraordinary intensive-care children who received extra help when they needed it and matured to become sources of strength for themselves and role models for others.

Chapter One

Strengthening Wings: Love and Appreciation

It is easier to build strong children than to repair broken men.

—Frederick Douglas

Over the past sixty years I have planted hundreds of plants and trees with limited success. One thing I can say, however, is that my success rate has increased with experience. I have learned that if I have a plan to control for water, sunlight, temperature, weed and fertilizer needs, my success rate goes way up. I believe that the same type of concern for basics can easily be applied to child-rearing. If parents and teachers have a plan and a commitment to provide their children with the important essentials necessary for healthy childhood growth and development, the chances of these children leading responsible and productive lives are greatly increased. In this chapter I will discuss the two elements of child-rearing that I consider to be of the utmost importance in our efforts to help our children "blossom" as independent and responsible adults. These elements include:

1. Unconditional love
2. Appreciating the miracle of learning

I. *Unconditional love*

> If you want to change the world, go home and
> love your family.
> —Mother Teresa

"I will love you when you are good, and I will love you when you are bad." What a powerful statement this is! It is also a statement that needs to be communicated by parents and teachers to children on a routine basis. Whether an adult actually says this magical statement or gives his son a hug after he spilled his soup on the floor, is of no importance. The main idea here is that unconditional love must be communicated to children in good and bad times. In his book, *Parenting from the Heart* (2012), Jack Pransky comments, *"What our children feel from us at the moment is the only thing that really matters."* The author is basically saying that our actions, words, and posturing convey a message to the child that greatly influences future responses by the child. One would hope that the message of love is always present in these parent/child communications even though feelings of disappointment and anger may appear from time to time. Accepting the fact that parents and teachers are human beings who sometimes let emotions get the best of them, it is very reassuring to know that the loving, postdisciplinary talk with a child can sometimes make up for a botched discussion earlier. This recovery plan worked for me more than once.

Your thirteen-year-old daughter wants to go to a party at a new friend's house. After doing a little checking with friends, you decide that this is not a good idea. Your denial explanation is met with some harsh words: "You are a terrible parent...you keep me captive in this prison you call a house!" Your gut tells you to fire back, but your mind tells you to use restraint. What will you do?

I believe the best approach in this situation would have been to say, "I understand your disappointment, but I love you, and for this reason, I cannot allow you to go to this party for your own safety." Hard as it is, the harsh adolescent comments should be ignored. Expressing love even in dire circumstances is a representation of unconditional love, and IT IS DIFFICULT TO DO. In a very keen sense, unconditional love is no more than following the Judea-Christian belief that Jesus represents love and sometimes we have to "turn the other cheek" to some pretty bad stuff in order to uphold the principle of unconditional love. Alfie Kohn, in his book, *Unconditional Parenting* (2005), points out that the children of abusive parents often display unconditional love for their abusive parents under the most terrible circumstances; it seems reasonable that parents from all makes of life would provide their children unconditional love as much as possible in a similar but more understandable manner.

Homes and classrooms with unconditional love are not lacking in accountability. In these settings *the behavior is judged, not the person.* That is to say, if the thirteen-year-old sneaks out, she may have to be on restriction for a week, but she will not be branded as mean, disrespectful or rebellious. "Focus upon the behavior" has to be the mantra of the adult who faces these challenges. In all cases, the adult responses to misbehavior will vary but the communication of love must remain steadfast.

"You scored above ninety on your spelling test, so you get ten dolphin dollars." This system of reinforcement for positive behavior in our schools has become the norm in most American elementary schools in the last decade. Sometimes known as PBS (positive behavior system), it is a behavior management system based upon Skinnerian principles. Sometimes this system influences student achievement and citizenship, but sometimes it does not. The staff implementing the system must make sure the rewards continue to please the children and the rewards are given on a routine basis with consistency. This PBS system has many advocates and few opponents. One antagonist of this rewards system, however, who has received quite a bit of attention in educational circles is Alfie Kohn, the author of *Unconditional Parenting* (2005).

In his book Kohn makes the case that parents and teachers who insist upon systematically rewarding good behavior are creating children who are driven by external rewards and not intrinsic motivation. Of greater concern, Kohn sees this overemphasis on performance rewards as creating children who have fragile self-concepts.

Kohn says, *"When children receive affection with strings attached, they tend to accept themselves only with strings attached."* This is an alarming statement because it suggests that conditional reward systems are damaging to the mental health of our children. The children who regularly earn performance rewards become dependent on performance to maintain their self-esteem; the children who do not earn Dolphin dollars often find themselves continually in a state of low esteem.

Clearly, it is important for all teachers and parents to reflect upon their interactions with children to make sure performance expectations never get in the way of genuine, unconditional love. As a sports enthusiast, I often appreciate the love of a parent comforting his child who just lost a game just as much, if not more, than the parent who is hugging his victorious child. The message is clear: *"I will love you whether you win or lose, whether you go to college or join the military or whether you graduate or drop out."*

Loving a child should not be a difficult thing for parents to do. For many young couples the birth of a child represents a time to care for, support, and connect with a beautiful little human being. The warm hugs, the bedtime stories, the playing catch in the backyard, and many other activities, are all experiences where true affection can be shared and enjoyed to the fullest depth of our collective soul. The Truckee River outside of my house roars in the fall, glimmers with snow in the winter, and slows to a creek in the summer, but there is one constant: it always flows. This is what unconditional love is all about: despite good and bad experiences in our lives, it must always flow.

II. Appreciating the miracle of childhood learning

> Parents can accept their child's invitation to slow
> down and appreciate the beauty and connection
> that life offers each day.
> —Siegal and Hartzell 2014

The importance of learning is often discussed in very general terms, but little attention has been placed upon the *miracle* of learning. To use a metaphor from the sports world, we may discuss a Michael Jordan dunk shot in terms of the two points scored and the score of the game, but the beauty of this superhuman man gliding through the air ten feet above the ground should not be overlooked. We never should ignore the beauty of a basketball dunk shot, nor should we ignore the majestic beauty of childhood learning. Milestones will happen, graduations will occur and careers will evolve, but the true beauty of these processes begins with appreciation for the wonders of childhood learning and personality unfolding.

An infant says, "Ma," and bells ring, calls to grandparents occur, and small family celebrations occur. Are these celebrations centered upon achievement and milestones, or are they celebrations of the miracle of learning? Probably, the answer to this question is "all of the above." Let us explore the miracle of learning a little more, for this is a phenomenon we should "step back" and appreciate throughout our lives.

At birth, the human brain is estimated to have somewhere in the vicinity of one hundred billion neurons that are not yet connected in networks (Shore 1997). It is the connecting of these neurons that forms the basis of human learning. For the child to recognize his mother, his sense of sight, smell, and memory must connect to see a pattern. Add to this equation the physiological and symbolic use of language, and "Ma" is the beautiful outcome. Millions of neurons and their hairlike connectors known as dendrites have come together in a pattern to help the infant say his first word. By the time children are three, their neuron connections in certain parts of the brain have doubled or even tripled depending upon genetics and environmental exposures the child has experienced (Medina 2008). This is an incredible feat that takes place in all children and continues throughout their lives. The importance of environmental experiences in this process can never be understated.

Every word a child learns, every new concept a child begins to understand and every lesson a child learns from a mistake is a *miracle to be appreciated*. The brain is constantly rewiring itself, and this "construction" project continues throughout our lives (Medina 2008). How exciting is this! It is also a message of *responsibility* to parents and teachers because we are important members of this construction team. Children who are exposed to learning activities and increased language opportunities tend to have brains with more neuron connections and greater adaptability to the learning require-ments of our society. This means that the field trips to the park, reading stories, and constant verbal interactions we are having with children are actually contributing to the structure of their brain. My wife, who constantly talked to our infant sons, was a construction engineer in disguise, and so are the many parents who take the time to engage their children in learning activities, read to them and speak with them throughout the day. We must take the time to understand our adult responsibilities and appreciate the miracle of childhood learning that we are privileged to witness and assist.

It is essential that we understand and appreciate the *uniqueness* of each child. No two children have the same brain paths and con-nections, nor do any two children have the same experiences in life. Equally important, it is essential that all parents and teachers recognize their responsibility to expose children to active learning opportunities that are the catalyst for neuron connections in the developing brain.

Recently, I was leading a guidance lesson with second graders at Mariposa Dual Language Academy in Reno about the importance of being kind to others. After finishing a reading of the book *Have You Filled a Bucket Today* (McCloud 2006), a little girl in the back row shyly raised her hand and stated, "When I fill my bucket up, I think I am going to share my bucket with other students who have empty buckets because it is important for everyone to have a full bucket."

I praised the little girl and used her response as a catalyst for fur-ther discussions about being kind to others. It was only later at lunch that I took a minute to reflect upon the amazing jump in abstract thinking this little girl had made and how this will affect her the rest of her life—it was awesome. *Just as important, I had taken the time over a peanut butter sandwich to appreciate the creativity of his child's beautiful mind. We must all learn to pause and reflect about the wonders of childhood learning.*

Chapter Two

Strengthening Wings: Critical Learning Activities

In the fall of each school year, most kindergarten teachers do an assessment of their incoming students to determine the needs of their new students. It is a very anxious moment for the parents and these five-year-olds visiting a school for the first time and meeting a "real" teacher. Most of the assessments involve a measure of language skills, prereading skills, motor skills, and a glimpse into the behavior and confidence of the child. In a nutshell, these assessments really provide a quick panoramic view of the learning activities these children have been exposed to in the early stages of their life. These assessments also provide predictions: some children will need lots of extra help in school to do well, and others are primed to be successful in school and prosperous in life. It is my contention that parents and preschool teachers who work with young developing children give them a big head start in life if they pay attention to certain basic learning activities that prepare these children to be successful in school. What type of learning activities are most beneficial to young, developing children who will be entering school at age five?

The broad answer(s) to this question are discussed in countless books about parenting and teaching that go into more depth than I am prepared to present. Nevertheless, I would like to focus upon three essential learning activities at home and in school that prepare students to be successful learners in life: *language, exploration, and reading.*

A. Language

> It's not the toys in the house that make the difference in children's lives; it's the words in their heads.
>
> —Jim Trelease 1996

In the 1930s H. M. Skeets and H. B. Dye (Heward 2000) did a study involving institutional children that is considered to be one of the great educational studies of all time. These researchers removed thirteen children considered to be "slow" from an orphanage and placed them in an institution for "mentally retarded" women. A control group of twelve orphaned children were left in the orphanage. One can assume that the children left in the orphanage had very little stimulation, whereas the children with the mentally retarded women were probably spoiled and talked to all the time. IQ testing that occurred two and a half years later showed that the children cared for in the institution gained twenty-eight points and the children left in the orphanage lost thirty points. What a remarkable study pointing to the relationship between family mental stimulation and mind capabilities! Who gained more value from the placement of these children with the mentally retarded women, the children or the women? I am going to say it was a tie because the women were helped to find more meaning in their lives, and the children's cognitive and language development was greatly enhanced.

Children who have strong language skills do better in school. This is an established fact that runs across all educational research. Language is the reference point for all reading and it is a prerequisite skill for conceptual understanding. It is so much easier to identify the word "elephant" in a story if I have learned about elephants in my home, and I have a reference point. Similarly, comparing a banana to an apple is a little difficult if I have never been exposed to the word "fruit." The examples can go on and on; we need language skills to do well in school and on the job. There are many papers written about strategies for language development in the home, but they usually "boil down" to *talk and listen* to your kids all the time. This means turning off the TV and spending time talking to your kids about their day. If the TV is on, talk to your kids about the lesson of a cartoon or the wonders of Nature on the National Geographic channel.

There is a sad reality in our society today that we must confront with the utmost commitment. Children living in poverty tend to have less exposure to words than their counter-parts in wealthy families, and this mere fact is putting these poor children at a tremendous disadvantage when they are entering school. Jessica Lahey, a writer for the Atlantic Magazine, provided this commentary in October of 2014:

> By the time these children are five years old, the poor ones will have heard thirty million fewer words than their wealthy peers.

Ms. Lahey continued in her article to highlight the disadvantage that language impoverished children have when they begin kindergarten. The most obvious solution to this dilemma is to educate and encourage *all* parents to speak, listen and read with their children. Secondly, programs like Head Start, designed to help low income children catch up in literacy and language, are a must in all walks of our society. I have to say I was very pleased in our State of Nevada when our education-oriented governor, Brian Sandoval, recently succeeded in legislating preschool grants to help low income four-year-olds have a year of instruction before kindergarten.

Teachers generally meet children at the schoolhouse door who have basic language skills, but it is their job to help students to enhance these skills to prepare students for a complex society. This challenge is, of course, much tougher when the children are second language students.

When I walked through classrooms as a principal, I looked for three elements that will always be indicators of good language development strategies used by teachers:

1. Was there a language focus (vocabulary discussions, words on the wall, etc.) throughout the classroom and teaching day?
2. Was there a high ratio of student vs teacher talk (kids need to talk and verbalize concepts)?
3. Were the teacher's words "think starters or think stoppers" (Hunter 1990)?

All three of these indicators involve the use of language as a platform to develop complex ideas and increased neuron connections in the maturing brain. Vocabulary development is the foundation for the platform and vocabulary expression becomes the driving force for complex ideation. If teachers become adept at asking open-ended questions (e.g., what would you have done if you were Harry Potter?) which provoke thinking, they will produce students who are better prepared for the academic and career challenges ahead. The teacher who asks this Harry Potter question will have succeeded in creating a "think starter" question that will cause a child or a class to engage in complex thinking, language expression and increased neuron connections.

When I was a graduate student taking a reading instruction class in the 1980s, I remember learning about the DRTA (directed reading thinking activities). This concept was so powerful to me then, and it maintains its importance forty years later. Simply put, the parent or teacher reading with a student stops his/her reading at key junctures and asks the child "think starter" questions. For example, when reading the story of *Cinderella*, a parent could ask her child, "Have you ever felt left out like Cinderella? Tell me what happened." Once again, the child is guided to use language as a tool for complex thinking. Reading becomes a thinking activity.

Parents, of course, can use the same techniques at home. This process begins with talking to your kids as much as possible. Taking the time to explore a word your child has heard in your conversation, on a billboard or on TV can have great impact on a child's vocabulary development. Finally, reading is the ultimate source of vocabulary development because the child is absorbing words and having fun without even noticing the process. Parents can use the DRTA technique to enhance the vocabulary and thinking benefits of a story.

B. Exploration

> A child in his earliest years, when he is only two or a little more, is capable of tremendous achievements simply through his unconscious power of absorption, though he is himself still immobile. After the age of three he is able to acquire a great number of concepts through his own efforts in exploring his surroundings. In this period he lays hold of things through his own activity and assimilates them into his mind.
> —Maria Montessori, *The Discovery of the Child*, translated by M. Joseph Costelloe, SJ

I believe Maria Montessori, better than most educational prophets, captured the eternal idea that children have a strong and desperate drive to learn and organize their observations into mindful concepts. This cannot be a foreign observation to anyone—just watch a toddler explore his environment in every detail.

Recently, I watched my nephew's one-year-old twins explore and play with every object in their grandmother's living room nonstop for an hour. The curiosity in their eyes, the fascination of touching things and the joy in their hearts was breathtaking. The light switch was just as important as the forty-dollar toy one twin played with, and I could tell the toy wrapping was next on his path. Jerome Bruner called this type of learning "discovery learning," whereas Maria Montessori would call it natural learning or absorption.

Parents and teachers have a role in this type of learning: set up a stimulating environment and get out of the way of the child. Let the child find meaning in his environment. There is nothing more stimulating than a trip to a park or museum to get things going for a child. Although it's best that the adult allows the child to lead his explorations, an occasional question or "Look at this" can be very helpful. Of course, discovery learning becomes a bit more structured as children get older and participate in science projects, field trips, travel, and developing recipes for making cakes. It is all about letting the child follow his natural need to learn and find meaning in his environment.

Discovery learning can manifest itself in many ways in schools. The basis of this approach to learning is to encourage the child to develop his own explanations of reality. Teachers who are trained well in the "Everyday Math" curriculum used in many schools often ask this question after a math problem has been presented: "Did anyone solve this problem in another way?" This question was always music to my ears as a principal because it invited the students to use their own approach to solving the problem.

Once in a while a parent has complained to me that he/she does not have the time or resources to go on field trip with his or her child. The answer to this concern is pretty simple—allow reading to be your field trip. All it costs is the time it takes to get a library card. Children love to be read to, and it is a great opportunity for children to go on imaginary field trips sitting on their parent's lap. The many benefits of reading aloud to children will be discussed in more depth in the next section.

C. Reading

> Education is not the filling of a bucket but the lighting of a fire.
> —William Butler Yeats

In my years as an educator and as a parent, I have been amazed by the joy children have when they are read to. There is no greater pleasure than holding a toddler in your lap and traveling on an imaginary journey into outer space or through a jungle with animal friends. The narrator and visitor buckle up, hold hands, and sail into a world traveled together. Imagination is set aglow, language skills are enhanced, prereading skills are developed, but most important, companionship is fostered. Reading to children of all ages can be a heartwarming experience that "lights the fire" of children.

Not only is reading to children fun and gratifying, we also know that reading skills are often a predictor of economic success in life for the children being read to. An impressive fifty-year study of seventeen thousand individuals in England, Scotland and Wales (Bates, Ritchie 2013) concluded that reading skill at the age of seven was a "key factor" in determining the later income level of these individuals. My observations lead to me believe that a comparable study would yield similar results in our country. Good readers usually do better in school which often opens the door to greater opportunities after school.

It's a rainy day, and your fifth grader is sitting in his room with nothing to do. Will he go downstairs to watch TV or will he pick up a chapter book adventure to read? Right now you are probably hoping the boy will go the reading route. Strange as it may seem, the choice the boy makes will be strongly affected by the reading experiences he had as a younger child. If he associated reading with fun, imagination and companionship, there is a good chance he will choose to read. Conversely, if reading was forced on him at a too rapid rate, the TV may be the choice. There is a simple message here for parents and teachers: If you want a child to be a life-long reader, take care to make the early childhood reading experiences fun and developmentally appropriate. There is nothing worse than forcing a child to read before he is ready to do so.

What is the best way to teach a child to read? It starts with reading aloud to the child. In 1985 the Federal government commissioned the "Becoming a Nation of Readers" report because of doubts about the efficacy of American educational institutions. One conclusion of this report was,

> The single most important activity for building the knowledge required for eventual success in reading is reading aloud to children.
> (*Becoming a Nation of Readers* 1985)

The report went on to say that reading aloud to children should continue throughout the grades. This is a recommendation I have never quivered with because I have witnessed, both as a parent and as a teacher, the state of wonder and amazement that overcomes children when they are read to. It is as if a magical spell overwhelms the children and allows their true imaginative and creative thought processes to emerge. Rarely have I ever met a child under the age of ten who did not enjoy being read to. Perhaps Jim Trelease (2013), a leading proponent for reading aloud, said it best when he highlighted the benefits of reading aloud to children:

- Build vocabulary.
- Condition the child's brain to associate reading with pleasure.
- Create background knowledge.
- Provide a reading role model.
- Plant the desire to read.

Many reading initiatives in 2017 focus upon *Guided Reading* (Fountas, Pinnel 1996) as the first reading strategy for all children. It is certainly not the only reading strategy to be used, but it is considered to be the core strategy and it is a strategy that can be used at home as well as school. In guided-reading groups the teacher reads to students, encourages the students to read silently and to each other, asks thoughtful questions, and keeps the story moving and exciting. The key features of guided reading are: grouping students by similar skills, teacher modeling of fluent reading and word strategies, DRTA activities, story enjoyment and assessment of individual reading skills. The goal of these Guided Reading activities is to help students develop independent reading skills with a focus upon the search for meaning in all passages to be read.

Parents can easily use guided-reading strategies in their homes to bond with children and increase their prereading skills. Planning thirty minutes of your day to spend quality reading time with your child is a gift to your child. According to a 1999 Department of Education Early Longitudinal Study (Trelease 2013), children who were read to at least three times a week were almost twice as likely to score in the top 25 percent in reading in their class. This is a statistical finding that is hard to ignore. Whether a parent spends thirty minutes a day reading with a child or ninety minutes a week, the return on this time investment for the child *and parent* can be incredible.

In summary, it is very evident to me that parents and teachers who encourage language development, reading, and exploration are providing their children with golden opportunities to expand their minds, enhance their imagination and prepare for successful school and career journeys. In a sense, these parents are preparing their children to "fly away" from their homes with the best possible wings.

Chapter Three

Strengthening Wings: Emotional Development

Educating the mind without educating the heart
is no education at all.

—Aristotle

L oving your child, appreciating your child, and providing your
child with bountiful learning activities should provide the right
foundation for your child to fly into his/her future with strong
wings, right? Not so fast, my own experiences and the observations
of several researchers would suggest that there are other parenting
and teaching behaviors that need to be considered.

Why is it that top ranked national schools such as Harvard and
Stanford review student applications to look for leadership experiences involving class offices, sports, community activities, and many
other activities? How is it that children who have a secure attachment
with their mother at age one are more likely to graduate from high
school (University of Minnesota Study 1970) The answer to these
two fundamental questions is, of course, that the emotional development of a person is a key factor in his/her educational, career and
life success.

In the past twenty years no author has done more to put a spot-
light on emotional development as a predictor of success in life than
Daniel Goleman (1998). The term "emotional quotient" (EQ) was
coined by Goleman to quantify "the capacity for recognizing our

own feelings and those of others, for motivating ourselves, and for managing emotions well in ourselves and in our relationships." In his research Goleman has discovered that EQ is a far better predictor of outstanding job performance than is IQ (Goleman 1998). In fact, Goleman suggests that IQ only accounts for about 25 percent of achievement.

I did not have to read Goleman's books to understand the importance of EQ. As a principal, I valued examples of collaboration on a résumé more than college GPA when I interviewed teacher candidates. *Similarly, I have observed over a forty-five-year career in education that the best teachers in a school are usually the most emotionally stable adults.* There is no question in my mind that emotional maturity is a big factor influencing career success and general happiness in life. In this section of the book I will discuss three aspects of childhood emotional development that I consider to be crucial to a child's success and happiness in life: (a) attachment, (b) self-awareness and self-control, and (c) empathy development.

A. Attachments

A two-week-old infant cries, and his mother warmly picks him up and soothes the baby with a bottle. It is this mother's response to the baby's needs that forms the basis of attachment theory. The mother sends a message of safety and loving to the baby that fills the baby with trust and frees the baby to explore his environment. Of course, there are many different types of attachments that the mother/infant can have, but the key feature of this attachment is caring, trust and safety. A child who is repeatedly denied the safety of a loving parent will soon learn his own defenses, and many times these defenses have a lasting effect that may not be advantageous for the child as he grows and develops. An infant who has a bottle stuck in his mouth with disdain over and over may grow up to have the same type of unloving attachment with his peers and cohorts. The quality of the relationship with the primary care-giver often plays a preeminent role in the personality development of the child.

As human beings, we tend to listen to and trust others who we perceive to care for us. I tend to believe that this variation of attachment theory is applicable in our lives well beyond infancy in homes, in schools, and on the job. Perhaps, Teddy Roosevelt said it best when he said the following:

> Students don't care how much you know until
> they know how much you care.

In 2004 the National Research Council determined that many school dropouts leave school because "they feel no one cares." There is a message here for all parents and educators: if you want to be listened to and if you want your children to do well in life, show your children that you care for them!

B. Self-Awareness and self-control

> Fish swim, birds fly and people feel.
> —Haim Ginott 2007

When a child falls off his bicycle on the first go-around, do we immediately lift him up and put him on the bicycle again with words of advice? No, we do not do this; instead, we comfort the child and encourage him before new instruction begins. The point here is we need to deal with the feelings of the child before we repeat the teaching process. Recognizing and responding to feelings prior to any form of instruction is an important thesis of Dr. Haim Ginott in his famous book *Between Parent and Child* (2007). The important message that Dr. Ginott and many other psychologists and counselors share with us is the fact that understanding, interpreting, and responding to the feelings of a child must take center stage in the parenting arena and classroom. Self-awareness is no more than the ability to recognize a feeling and interpret it to oneself and to others.

Teaching a child or student to be self-aware, of course, begins with the self-awareness of the adult and the ability of the adult to model self-awareness. There are no substitutes for this key feature of parenting and teaching. How valuable it is when an adult says, "I am really angry right now, so I am going to take a break before I make a decision." It is important for adults to model and teach a feeling vocabulary to children, so that they, too, may someday recognize their own feelings and communicate these feelings to others in an appropriate manner.

In my years as a school psychologist, I often was asked to deal with young communication-delayed children with behavior problems. Soon I began to realize that these children were acting out their emotions because they had no means to express their feelings when they were upset. With the help of committed speech-language therapists, caring teachers and involved parents, several of these students improved their behavior as their expressive language improved. I did learn a valuable lesson as a young psychologist: feeling awareness and expression is often related to student behavior.

I think it would be fair to say that self-awareness is not an end in itself. The self-control that must follow self-awareness is the next step in the process of developing emotional maturity. Remember, in the example cited above the adult took a "break" after he recognized he was angry. Parents and teachers are wise to model good self-control behaviors and attempt to teach them to children. I like to think of self-control as a menu of choices we have when we have a strong emotion. For example, when a teacher is angry with one of her students, she can take a few breaths and calm herself down, walk around the room, yell at the student to relieve her tension, or choose to ignore the student and help another student. The hope is that that the teacher will recognize her anger, take measures to calm herself down and deal with the student's misbehavior in a purposeful manner. A similar menu of choices would be available to a parent who is extremely mad at his or her child. Children are always watching and learning from their parents' and teachers' examples of good and bad self-control.

C. Empathy

No one has fully realized the wealth of sympathy, kindness and generosity hidden in the soul of a child. The effort of every educator should be to unlock that treasure.

—Emma Goldman

Empathy is the act of trying to understand another person's feelings or as often said, "putting yourself in another person's shoes." I describe empathy as an action because the empathetic person must truly listen to another person, watch his/her nonverbal expressions and attempt to interpret these feelings. It is a complex process that begins with an attitude that drives a person to *want* to understand another person.

Perhaps, empathy can best be understood when we look at the absence of empathy. Severely autistic children, through no fault of their own, generally have a lack of empathy that makes it very difficult to function in our society. The same absence of empathy rears its ugly head in sociopaths who often do cruel things to others because they cannot "feel" the pain they are creating. Most of us stand somewhere on the empathy continuum somewhere between 0 and 10 depending upon our experiences and upbringing. The important news is that a higher empathy score often correlates with better career and life satisfaction.

I will never forget the time when, as a school psychologist, I was invited by our principal into a meeting to discuss a student I had evaluated. After the team had reached a decision about an intervention, the principal, Ron, looked at me and said, "Doug, you look annoyed by this decision, please share with us your concerns." I was "taken aback" by this request, and I felt so honored that the principal would scan my facial expressions and care about my feelings and ideas enough to slow the meeting down. This was an example of empathy at play in a very important meeting leading to better decisions. More important, a young psychologist who would later become a principal had learned a valuable lesson that would become a tool in his playbook for years to come.

Common sense and experience tells me that people with high levels of empathy are happier in life because they are cared for. It does not take a rocket scientist to figure out that people who genuinely care for others by demonstrating empathy have more people caring for them. It is also not a surprise to me that empathy is a key variable predicting career success in many fields. Stephen Covey in his book *The 7 Habits of Highly Effective People* (2005) talks about "empathic listening" when he discusses habit five, "Seek first to understand, then to be understood." It is very interesting that Covey describes empathic listening as originating with an attitude of really *wanting* to understand another person's position on an issue or situation and using subtle skills such as active listening and reading body language to enhance one's understanding.

I like to read research studies that are longitudinal and have large sample sizes. For good reason, these studies have more relevance to me. A 2011 study in *Child Development* magazine explored the effects of empathic learning programs on 270,000 students. The students with this training had better social and emotional skills than their counterparts who did not receive the training. Surprisingly, these same students had an eleven point increase in standardized achievement scores. This is why empathy training is a big part of the guidance program I deliver weekly in a local charter school.

How is empathy taught to children? I think we all know the answer to this question. It is, of course, the modeling of empathy. Parents and teachers who model empathy on a day-to-day basis raise empathetic children and students. Taking the time to connect with your children or spouse regarding their feelings about a situation is golden in the annals of raising empathetic children. Fran Walfish (*Tough Love* 2016), a school psychologist and family psychotherapist, talks about the "empathic narration" as an essential strategy for adults to use when conversing with children. This term essentially means showing your child that you understand her feelings. This is not easy but it involves keenly listening to a child and attempting to understand the emotion of a child. The part of empathic narration that has always been a struggle for me is *putting aside solutions to problems in order to better focus upon the emotions of the problem*—it is challenging for adults to do and it takes practice. Dr. Walfish offers the following tips for "ensuring empathetic learning":

1. See your child for who he or she is, warts and all. Say to her, No one is perfect," then own up to your own errors when you make them. This will help your child accept herself, flaws and all

2. Empathize out loud to narrate your child's struggle in the moment. You could say, "It's really hard when you try your best and do not make it on the team," in a kind, compassionate, empathetic tone.

3. Be kind to your child while balancing empathic nurturing with firm boundaries. Even when you have to say no and your child fights you, stay kind and respectful. Never lose your cool and attack back.

4. Feel empathy for yourself, so you can feel empathy for your child. Accept the fact you will make mistakes. We are all on a learning curve, but the key is to acknowledge your mistakes, own up to them, and start over. "Oops, there I go again," as you own up to your misstep, can go a long way. In this way you are modeling empathy for your own imperfections.

5. Recognize your own level of empathy, even though this is easier said than done. Lack of empathy is a classic sign of self-absorption. Is it in you to automatically think about the impact of your words and behavior on other people? If not, use empathic narration on yourself. Over time you will begin to see yourself in the shoes of others, and can instill this very important personality trait in your children. (*Tough Love*, 139)

Practicing empathy in homes is a wonderful gift to children; practicing empathy in the classroom is an essential element in the quest to develop prepared and successful citizens in our society. The teacher who takes the time to daily greet her students, care about the emotional struggles of their little lives and listen to their stories is delivering a powerful message of empathy in a world that sometimes can be very insensitive to the needs of our children.

Chapter Four

Strengthening Wings: Empowerment and Uniqueness

When I approach a child he inspires in me two sentiments:
Tenderness for what he is and respect for what he may become.

—Louis Pasteur

I. Empowerment

When a bear cub is finally released from his mother, he must have the courage, preparation and self-confidence to go it alone. Although the human version of bear separation is less abrupt, it still occurs over time. Books are written about the preparation for adulthood, but in this narrow context I prefer to write about the courage and self-confidence *attitudes* that are vital elements in the transition away from home and into adulthood. In this chapter I will call the courage to attempt something and the self-confidence to follow through an attitude of *empowerment*. I believe that there are three factors that add together to create empowerment: choices, responsibility and success:

Choices

It's 8:00 a.m., and a busy mother is preparing her toddler to go to day care. She puts out three pairs of socks and asks the child to pick the pair she wants to wear. Although this step drains three minutes of "out-the-door" time, the mother believes it is a valuable exercise. Why? This mother is infusing "choice" into her daughter's life whenever she can. This strategy carries an important message to the child: "You are important and capable of making important choices in your life."

Giving children choices is an essential element of effective parenting and teaching. I am often reminded of a simple quote by Alfie Kohn (Unconditional Parenting 2005) that sticks in my mind: "*The way kids make good decisions is by making decisions.*" We must let children become decision-makers at a very early age. Notice that the aforementioned parent did limit her child's choices to three because she was not prepared to have her child wear a polka dot sock with a plaid green sock. The parental limits on child decisions must be loosened as children become teenagers, but parents always have a right to limit the range of choices based upon safety and agreed upon family values.

I will never forget a situation in our home involving my sixth-grade son and safety patrol. He repeatedly made the decision to dawdle and delay getting ready for his early patrol duty. We became tired of rushing him along and furiously driving to school to get him at his street position on time. Finally, after much discussion, we told him that we would not supervise him getting ready for patrol, nor would we drive him if he was late. He would have to make the choice to prepare himself and get to his position on time. The first time he failed we kept our side of the bargain and did not drive him. It hurt us a great deal watching him leave the door late in tears, but we wanted him to face the consequences of his decisions. He was suspended from patrol for a week.

If we encourage our children to make choices and decisions, we must allow these children to live with the consequences of their decisions. This does not mean walking away from the decisions; instead, it means standing on the sidelines, encouraging our children and consoling them in a helpful manner when things do not go well.

I often walk in Idlewild Park along the Truckee River in Reno. One day I noticed a grove of cottonwood trees had been planted near the walk path. Interestingly, each young tree had a five-foot stake driven in the ground next to it with a wire connected to the tree. Each stake was in the ground to support a tree. The tree could waver in the wind and gain and lose its leaves, but it always would have the support of the solemn stake that stood strong in the ground. One day the trees will outgrow their stakes, but for now, those stakes are very vital to the young trees. Parents can be the stakes that support children when they make good and bad decisions.

Children who have choices in life are emboldened to become decision-makers as adults. Sometimes their decisions go well and sometimes their decisions do not go well. The important thing is that these children are empowered to take control of their lives, and they have learned that they can survive poor decisions and reload to make good decisions.

Responsibilities

> Never do anything for a child that he can do for himself.
>
> —Many child experts

As I was helping primary students line up following an assembly at Mariposa Academy, a little hand touched my belt. A shy first grader with sparkling eyes looked up at me and said, "Mr. W, I am the line leader and the kids are supposed to line up behind me."

I quickly moved out of the way to let this little girl do her job. Similar to Alfie Kohn's statement about decisions, one could easily say that you cannot have responsible children unless you give them responsibilities—and this little girl was being responsible.

Stephen Glenn and Jane Nelsen (2000) do an excellent job pointing out that the shift in American society from a rural agricultural society prior to World War II to an urban industrial society has had a huge impact on families. Children on farms had to be up with the sun to feed the livestock, milk the cows and they took time off from school to harvest crops. This same level of family responsibility is certainly not the norm today. One can easily say that nowadays few children have meaningful responsibilities in their homes, and these children are often denied the opportunity to take on responsibility and to feel a part of something bigger than themselves like the family harvest.

Parents and teachers who want their children to be responsible must pay attention to the simple but intuitive statement that *childhood responsibilities create responsible adults*—it can't get much simpler than that! This means assigning chores, including children as a part of the "family team" and expecting results.

The tasks that parents and teachers assign to their children must be meaningful and within the child's capabilities. Just as you would not ask a four-year-old to watch the baby, you would not ask a sixth grader to referee a fifth-grade intramural basketball game. The maturity and skills of a child must be taken into account when assigning responsibilities to children. Furthermore, the adults assigning tasks to children must coach the children on how to do the tasks well. This "coaching" may be harder than doing the task yourself, but the dividends for the child of having successfully completed the task are too important to pass up on.

Forgive me for telling a story here, but this was one of many memorable stories I have experienced in my educational career. I remember a single-parent mother who had a sixth-grade and a second-grade student in our school. It's fair to say that these children were pretty spoiled because the mother did everything for her kids. One day the mother had an accident and broke her leg. Guess who had to do the cooking, dishes, and clothes washing? Her daughter and son were quite capable of doing these tasks with some coaching from their mother on the couch. To make a long story short, the accident caused the mother to learn about the capabilities of her kids, and she reported to me how impressed she was with their new sense of responsibility for themselves and the family. The benefit went two ways—the sixth grader seemed to handle her school responsibilities much better during her mother's rehabilitation. The lesson here is that adults should challenge their children to take on meaningful responsibilities in the home at an early age because this is part of the empowerment process that leads to successful adulthood.

Most school mission statements include the term "good citizen" somewhere in their text. The implication of this wording is that the role of our school is meant to go well beyond student achievement and test scores. One could make a good argument that preparing students to be good citizens means giving each child responsibilities and helping these children to see that they are a member of a valuable team bigger than themselves—the classroom. My little sparkly-eyed first grader was a student in a classroom where classroom duties were chosen weekly and the teacher often had classroom meetings to emphasize the responsibility of each student to her classmates as a team.

I am often reminded of the one-room schoolhouse that we saw as children watching *Little House on the Prairie* on our black-and-white TVs. Every child in the school had responsibilities and the big kids often helped the younger students with their studies. Some students cut wood for the fire, other students shoveled the snow on the pathways and almost everyone tutored a student younger than themselves. By necessity, attendance at the school meant responsibility training in action. It is true that many of the principles that formed the foundation of the one-room school houses are now being heralded in multiroom urban schools as principles to be followed in a different format—this is why we have line leaders in the first grade.

It is very evident that both parents and teachers have the opportunity to provide children with responsibilities at a very early age. Many times these adults choose not to assign children responsibilities for a variety of reasons. We have all heard statements such as, "I want my child to have it better than I did," or teachers lamenting that "class meetings take time away from math instruction." In these cases it is important to help these adults recognize that providing responsibilities to children in school and in home is a necessary gateway to empowerment and successful adulthood.

Success

> However bad life may seem, there is always some-
> thing you can do and succeed at. While there's
> life, there is hope.
>
> —Stephen Hawking

In the world of sports there is an accepted belief that "success builds success." For example, a team that plays a winning game on Saturday is more likely to practice hard the next week and increase their chances to win another game the following week. In a similar manner, a student who gets an A on a spelling test one week is more likely to study hard for the next test. Whether one calls this success story an application of Skinner's behavior reinforcement principles or fulfillment of Maslow's needs theory (self-esteem) is of no matter. The bottom line is that humans have a self-esteem need and feel better when they succeed at what they are doing. This is especially true for children, and it is critical that parents and teachers understand this. Success leads to confidence which, in turn, leads to empowerment. In this section of the chapter I will focus upon three elements of individual success: realistic expectations, adult support and child strengths.

When I was a coach of a high school basketball team in Delta Junction, Alaska, that had very little talent, I was challenged to help my players feel successful when their record was 0-10. My center that year was smaller than the guards of most teams and most of our players were just learning the game. Recognizing that I had to redefine success in realistic ways that could be achieved, we would set goals for each game such as ten assists or 38 percent shooting that motivated us during the games and in practice. We knew we could not win many games, but we needed to feel some levels of success in order to continue striving to improve as a team.

This Alaska story is an example *of redefining success* that many adults must do to help their children achieve success. The Learning Disabled student may be better served if his goal on a spelling test is to get half of the words correct on a shorter spelling test. Similarly, the obese junior high student may strive to run a fifteen-minute mile at the start of the season with a goal of running a fourteen-minute mile at the end of the running season. Hopefully, both the LD student and the obese student can take some pride in their accomplishments and strive to improve their records. *This principle of redefining success is basically creating reasonable expectations for children and celebrating their accomplishments. It is an adult position that puts a greater emphasis upon individual effort and progress than grades or winning games.*

Have you ever listened to a college sports coach talk to his team at halftime? These coaches are focused upon success and winning because their livelihood depends upon it. It does seem to me that parents and teachers would be wise to learn from some of the very best coaches who must teach success if they are to keep their jobs. I have observed (three) main strategies used by most successful coaches: passionate encouragement, reframing the game, and skill focus. These same strategies can be used by parents and teachers to help children find success in their endeavors.

There is nothing that comes easier to me than encouragement because it is so easy to do. I think I had encouraging parents and some outstanding coaches and teachers who inspired me to do well. They celebrated my successes with me and constantly told me that "I could do it." When you encourage a child in a passionate manner, you are helping this child to find the "power within his soul" to give his very best in whatever endeavor he is attempting. Whether it is winning the soccer game or getting an A on a spelling test, adult encouragement is an incredible instrument of love and success that is rewarding, potent and easy to do.

The simple action of reframing a situation can be a powerful motivator for a child. "I know you are disappointed with a C on your math test, but your score this week was higher than last week and you seem to have mastered adding fractions." These encouraging words by a math teacher to a struggling student can make the difference between a math "dropout" and a student who passes his proficiency test.

Encouragement and reframing situations in a positive manner are valuable strategies for teachers and parents to use to motivate students, but they are not sufficient for success. The missing ingredient is skill building. The teacher who helped her math student to see his C grade in a different light may also have offered to help the student with decimals after school. The basketball coach whose team is losing by thirty points must also coach the team on their skills. Their shots were too early, their defense needed to become more aggressive and the ball has to go to number 10 more often. Focusing upon helping a child with the skills she needs to be successful with her chores, her school work and her first job is a dimension of parenting that can never be underestimated.

Parents and teachers must make every effort to help their children to be successful in life endeavors. This means understanding the strengths/weaknesses of a child, providing the extra help the child needs to master skills and spending time encouraging and providing perspective to help the child find success. With each success the child becomes empowered to try harder and take chances in life.

This discussion of the need for success cannot end without a discussion of the *dangers* that may befall a child if he finds no success at school or at home. If one accepts the belief that we all need to have success and significance in life, it is easy to understand why some children turn to gangs or crime in order to find success. This may be a natural fallback position that occurs for children desperately searching for success at anything in their lives. As my good friend Terry has often said, *"The other team is always recruiting."* We must do everything we can to prevent this from happening by helping students to be successful at school, in the home or in the community.

II. Supporting and celebrating your child's uniqueness

Kahlil Gibran (1932) in *The Prophet* eloquently described the sanctity of childhood uniqueness when he wrote,

> Your children are not your children
> They are the sons and daughters of Life's Longing
> for itself.
> They come through you but not from you,

And though they are with you yet they belong
not to you
You may give them your love but not your
thoughts,
for they have their own thoughts.
You may house their bodies but not their souls,
For their souls dwell in the house of tomorrow,
which you cannot visit,
not even in your dreams.
You may strive to be like them, but seek not to
make them like you.
For life goes not backward nor tarries with
yesterday.
You are the bows from which your children as
living arrows are set forth.
The archer sees the mark upon the path of the
infinite, and He bends you with His might that
his arrows may go swift and far.
Let your bending in the archer's hand be for
gladness;
For even as He loves the arrow that flies, so He
loves the bow that is stable.

What a beautiful poem by Kahlil Gibran! I wish I had kept this poem close to my heart when my wife and I were raising our young boys. *It reminds us that our children have their own spirit, their own minds and their own destiny, but we have a charge to keep our guiding bow steady.* Part of our steadying influence is to make the supreme effort to understand and value the uniqueness of our children. This journey begins with an attitude of appreciation of the individuality of our children and an understanding that our children cannot and need not mirror ourselves. A beginning point for this journey is to make an effort to understand a child's strengths and weaknesses and, more importantly, to help each child understand the same.

BASIC IDEAS AND STRATEGIES TO HELP PARENTS AND EDUCATORS RAISE SUCCESSFUL CHILDREN WITH INNER DISCIPLINE

A. Child strengths

Michael Phelps, the most decorated Olympic athlete in American history, was a lousy student who had a hard time concentrating in class. Recognizing that every child needs to feel success, his mother enrolled him in swimming classes. We all know the rest of the story! The lesson learned here is that every child has strengths and every child needs successes. Mrs. Phelps recognized that she would need to encourage Michael to pursue swimming, his area of strength, because he was spending 50 percent of his day in a school environment where he struggled to feel any success at all. Teachers and parents are wise to really understand their children and put on their "strength-finder" lenses to help children discover their own strengths and to begin the process of cultivating these strengths. Marcus Buckingham and Donald Clifton in their book, *Now, Discover Your Strengths* (2001), have a wonderful quote that should have meaning to most parents and teachers trying to help children find success in life:

> The real tragedy of life is not that each of us doesn't have enough strengths; it's that we fail to use the ones we have. Benjamin Franklin called wasted strengths "sundials in the shade."

We must all dedicate ourselves to help the children we work and live with to find their strengths and be able to use them. This may mean asking the poor reader in your class to be a math tutor, taking your child who struggles in school to ballet classes, or having your most troubled student be office messenger. Whether one calls it cultivating strengths or finding significance, it is so important that we allow children to do what they are good at and celebrate their accomplishments.

I will never forget Paul. He was a fifteen-year-old sophomore on my Delta High basketball team in Alaska. At the age of seven, a truck had collided with the family car Paul was a passenger in. Paul's parents were killed, but he survived with a metal plate in his brain. Paul was very intellectually delayed, but he was a gifted athlete. It was my job to mold Paul into a high school basketball player. He could never learn a play, but he looked like "Earl the Pearl" on a fast break and could score baskets. I made the decision to keep Paul on our team and insert him into the lineup when the pace of games picked up. The other players knew he could not run a play, but they appreciated his fast break moves and understood he would never participate in a set play. My "strength-finder" lens and the incredible understanding of his teammates had allowed Paul to be successful in a very important activity in his life. When Paul was a senior, we were able to get him a job at our local fast food place washing dishes. He could never tell you what 2+2 was, but he could wash four dishes in the time it takes to go down the court for a score. I am not sure if Paul was ever able to cognitively understand that his strengths were in the motor areas, but I do know that if you ever needed to find him, he would be in the gym.

B. Child weaknesses

Just as it is important to learn about and appreciate a child's strengths, it is equally important to understand and respond to each child's weaknesses.

As a school psychologist, I was asked to do an evaluation of a fourth grader who was getting Cs and Ds in reading at a local elementary school. These grades were not that remarkable; what was remarkable was that she had always received A grades in reading prior to the third grade. The parents blamed their child for laziness, and they were very frustrated with her grades. After about three hours of assessment and discussion with the girl, I had a hypothesis about what was going on. The little girl had outstanding strengths with memory tasks, but she was significantly below average in tasks requiring abstract thinking. My hypothesis was that this little girl was at a disadvantage as the school curriculum was becoming more abstract. The memorizing that had helped this child become a fluent reader was not helping her with abstract tasks in the fourth grade when the teacher would ask for comparisons, summaries and lessons learned from passages.

Following the conclusion of our meeting, I believe the parents felt guilty about how they had treated their daughter but hopeful she could now receive the help she needed to do better in school. We did develop a plan to give her extra help with tasks requiring abstract thinking, and the teacher did modify her assignments in order to help her be more successful in school.

The lesson learned with this child was that the adults in her life failed to recognize that she had a learning weakness that required extra help and some accommodations. It is difficult for children to be successful in school if their academic needs are not addressed properly.

Last year I worked with a group of high school students with special needs at Bishop Manogue Catholic High School in Reno. The majority of the students were diagnosed with ADHD-type symptoms including distractibility and poor organization. Our students managed to earn about a 3.1 GPA in a college prep school because we gave them an extra four hours a week of organization and academic assistance. Some of their parents lamented the fact that they had to be involved with their child's school work at the ages of sixteen and seventeen when most parents of students had removed themselves from this task years earlier. My response to these parents was usually pretty simple: "Your son has unique needs that require that you stay involved with his school work much longer than normal."

The extra help a student needs in school from teachers and parents should not be based upon the student's age; instead, it should be based upon the student's needs. This process begins with an *adult mind-set* that accepts the idea that their children will often need to be treated differently based upon their demonstrated needs.

C. Self-understanding

Many times I have sat down with unmotivated students in school and asked them what they are good at. More often than not, these students with low self-esteem struggle to describe their strengths as human beings. This moment of silence has always been sad to me, but it is also diagnostic. It tells me that the parents and teachers of this child need to help the child to recognize his strengths and weaknesses as a person. Parents and teachers understanding the strengths of a child is not an end in itself; the real end is for the *child* to understand his strengths and weaknesses. This is a process that is not just reserved for children; it is a process that most of us will spend a lifetime grappling with. Just as all of us need to use our strengths as much as possible, we must also learn to accommodate our weaknesses.

I have had two rounds of chemo, and I am approaching my seventies. It is very evident to me that my short-term memory is diminished similar to many learning disabled students. My solution to this challenge is to demand of myself and the teachers I work with that everything that needs to be remembered must be written down. This is an accommodation I make for myself based upon a learning challenge—it works pretty well.

A similar accommodation might be made for a memory-challenged ninth grader trying to prepare for a biology test. This student may need a copy of the teacher's study guide or he may need to be able to tape the lectures because he cannot remember everything that was said. The key issue is whether or not the student will advocate for himself and ask for such notes. *Such advocacy will only occur if the student understands himself, accepts his weaknesses and is willing to ask for accommodations. We all must learn certain concepts in school, but the path each of us takes to do this learning does not have to be the same.*

Chances are that the ninth-grade biology student who needs accommodations to do well in the biology class has struggled to do well in school. One can only hope that his recognition of his memory deficit is matched by his understanding of his strengths as a person. You do not have to have a good memory to be a great artist, athlete, orator or mathematician (with a calculator). The most important element of this student's personal insight is the influence of parents and teachers who have hopefully never stopped emphasizing the strengths of this fourteen-year-old student. This discussion brings to mind a verse of a song I ran across:

"See Me Beautiful"
by Red and Kathy Grammer

See me beautiful
Look for the best in me
It's what I really am
And all I want to be
It may take some time
It may be hard to find
But see me beautiful
(*Teaching Peace*, RedNote Records)

Chapter Five

Strengthening Wings: Review and Reflect

The metaphor of the plant growing is so relevant to human development. If a proper foundation for the plant's roots is not provided to the plant, gardeners like me will spend hours later trying to help the plant survive, regardless of whether or not it blooms one day. Similarly, a child who is not provided a proper foundation in her childhood is at a disadvantage during her lifetime. The challenge to help this child find a way to "bloom" is much more difficult. Parents and teachers must do their very best to provide each and every child a good foundation to grow upon.

In chapters 1 to 4, parents and teachers were reminded to unconditionally love their children and to "*take a moment to enjoy a moment*" (Citibank ad 2018) in the lives of their children. This means taking pause in our busy days to appreciate the learning and love that are children so beautifully provide us.

Because the brain is a constantly evolving organ in our body, the importance of "fueling" this brain by providing children with language, reading and exploration activities was highlighted in some depth. Every time a child participates in a complex activity such as reading, the brain is challenged to rewire itself to accommodate new learning and, by doing this process, the brain becomes more adapted to meet the complexities of our society.

Researchers in the last few decades have studied human success and concluded rather strikingly that having an advanced brain is not sufficient to predict success in life. Instead, these researchers have underscored the prominence of emotional maturity in predicting success and happiness in life. The most important task for adults attempting to help their children mature emotionally is to demonstrate this emotional maturity themselves. This is not an easy task, and it may require help. The starting point for this process is the recognition that the behavior I model to my children will probably be the behavior they learn the easiest.

Lastly, children with strong wings have an attitude of empowerment and an understanding of themselves that allows them to take charge in their life. These are the individuals who had responsibilities and choices to make as children and have now become decision-makers as adults. They are not afraid to make a decision, and they have had enough success in life to feel confident they can make the right decision or recover if they make the wrong decision. They understand themselves and can move toward their strengths and manage their weaknesses.

Reflections

Strengthening the wings of children by providing them with the right foundation is a daunting task for parents. Sometimes we will be very effective in some areas and not so effective in other areas. The challenge is to do our best, keep learning, and take a moment to review our parenting progress.

Some questions parents and teachers may wish to ask themselves include the following:

- Is my message of *unconditional love and care* apparent to the children I live and work with at all times? Do I need to have more one-on-one discussions or take important actions to make sure this message is properly communicated?
- Is childhood *choice* encouraged in my home or in my classroom? Are children allowed to accept the responsibility of their choices within limits?

- Are children given responsibilities in the home and class-room that they are capable of completing successfully? Do the children have opportunities to be part of the "family or classroom team"?
- Parents: Are you reading with your young children at home on a consistent basis? Is the reading made fun and are you asking "thinking "questions? Are you turning off the TV to model adult reading habits?
- Teachers: Is your reading instruction tailored to meet the different skill levels children present in your class? Is the text students are reading interesting and thought provoking? Are you using proven reading instruction methodology?
- Are children encouraged to use their language skills often? Do teachers and parents *listen* to their children and ask "think-starting" questions often?
- Is childhood exploration encouraged in homes and in classrooms?
- Are you *modeling* empathy and consideration for others in your daily life? Are your children being exposed to a *feeling vocabulary?* Do you ever question what it would be like to be in the other person's shoes?
- Are you encouraging each child to find his or her strengths and providing opportunities for these strengths to be used? Are you helping children to better understand and appreciate themselves?
- Can the children in your home or in your classroom proudly describe what makes them unique?
- Are you taking the time to pause and celebrate the spirit, kindness, love, and creativity of children as they progress in life?

Chapter Six

The Inside-Out Approach

Successful parenting and teaching begins with
the parent and the teacher.

—Doug Whitener

T he major premise of this chapter is the idea that adults do a better job teaching when they are balanced, comfortable with themselves and focused upon their mission as parents and as teachers.
This is not a task to be completed; instead, it is a life-long process
that demands continual attention. Listed below are five major areas
of focus that each of us would be wise to place on our dashboard as
we travel through life as individuals first and as educators of children
second:

1. Understand and reflect about your childhood experiences.
2. Become mindful of our past.
3. Be a good model for your children.
4. Cut yourself some slack and develop a support system.
5. Sharpen the saw.

It is my observation, unsupported by data, that the majority of
effective educators in homes and in school are healthy, balanced individuals. They understand themselves, know what forces drive them
moment to moment and can adapt to situations by keeping a focus

upon their purpose. These individuals have developed an "inside-out" (Covey 1989) approach to life that is very apparent in their actions. That is to say, they have established a positive balance in their own life before they have tried to help others lead better lives. The rest of this chapter is designed to help the reader better understand the "inside-out" (IO) approach as it relates to educating children.

1. Understand and reflect about your childhood experiences

> Making sense of your life is the best gift you can
> give to your child.
> —Siegal and Hartzell 2014

Your eleven-year-old son has just had his birthday in July, and he is now eligible to play Pop Warner football this fall. Trying not to be overenthusiastic about this opportunity, you approach your son and matter-of-factly remind him that sign-ups are next week. Much to your disappointment, he shares that he is not interested in playing football. All sorts of thoughts go through your mind:

- My touchdown against the Eagles in sixth grade.
- How my parents bragged about my football.
- High school football and the cheerleaders' adoration.
- Will neighbor Jim Smith's son play football?
- Watching pro football games with my dad.
- Football scholarship to USC.

As the female teacher of a suburban sixth-grade classroom, you expect all students to be respectful to you in a manner similar to what your parents doggedly required. You never lose sight of the fact that you had to work very hard for your grades in school. After confronting a new student about not doing her homework, the student says, "I am not going to do this stupid homework!" All sorts of thoughts go through your mind:

- Good girls do not disrespect their parents or teachers ever.

- Good girls do their homework.
- I am a success in life because I did my homework.
- Students who do not do their homework are lazy and doomed for failure.

Okay, you know where I am going with these two scenarios. *How we were raised has a huge impact on how we parent and teach.* There is nothing wrong with this reality as long as we are aware of this phenomenon and we are willing to continually reflect about this powerful influence on our lives. Our family experiences should be one influence in our decision-making, not the controlling influence. That is to say, the disappointed father will need to step back and remember that his childhood experiences with football were positive, but not necessarily the best road for his son to take. Similarly, the sixth-grade teacher may need to step back and recognize that not all children are raised with the same commitment to school and respect that she was raised with.

2. Become mindful of our past

> All conversations are with myself, and sometimes they involve other people.
> —Scott 2002

It may be that our football father and motivated sixth-grade teacher cannot ever banish the childhood family experiences from affecting their perceptions about events. This being the case, how does one move on to become a better parent or teacher? The answer to this question involves understanding the concept of "mindfulness" (Siegel and Hartzell 2014). In the context of this chapter, "mindfulness" means the ability to reflect about one's past, judge the merit of our experiences as they relate to the present situation and never lose sight of the child's needs, experiences and aspirations. I believe this concept of "mindfulness" is best described below (Siegal and Hartzell 2014):

When we are mindful, we live in the present moment and are aware of our own thoughts and feelings and are also open to those of our children.

Our "mindful" football father may need to come to grips with his disappointment in his son's choices, explore his son's interests a bit more in conversation and try to find another activity he can support his son's involvement in. The sixth-grade teacher may need to gather herself, fight off her instant rage about the disrespect, and begin to try to understand this child's world. In both cases the adult will need to recognize his/her feelings, reflect upon his/her perspective, and listen to the child's story in an unbiased manner. In essence, both adults needed to have a conversation with themselves before they had a conversation with their children. The childhood experiences of these adults are not unimportant, but they should not be controlling, either; the child's world is the controlling factor.

I often wondered why I was reluctant during my early days as a principal to spend a lot of time in the kindergarten room of Lemmon Valley Elementary School. This was true despite the fact that kindergarteners are always the cutest kids in the school and we were blessed with good kindergarten teachers. This unwillingness to go in the kindergarten classes bothered me enough that I forced myself to reflect upon my past to see if there were any childhood experiences that would have caused me to avoid the kindergarten room. There was, indeed, an answer to this question hidden in my past, and I needed to have a conversation with myself.

My mother was a good mother who, like all parents, had her ups and downs as a parent. Her values remain a positive influence on my life today, but one of her faults was the manner in which she struggled with chaos. My three sisters and I learned to stay away from mother when things were chaotic because it could became somewhat dangerous. We developed a coping mechanism to avoid pain by separating ourselves from our mother during times of disarray that I believed flowed into other parts of our lives. I began to wonder if my dislike of chaos and my avoidance strategy was causing my unwillingness to regularly visit the kindergarten classrooms. This was my hypothesis, and I had to do something about it.

I needed to reorganize my thoughts about chaos in a manner that would allow me to carry out my responsibilities as a principal for all children, including kindergarteners. I gradually learned to respect the "organized chaos" that most kindergarten classes exhibit in a manner that fits the developmental needs of five-year-olds. It really helped me to play with some of the children in the play kitchen, and I appreciated the teacher's explanation of the learning that was occurring as the children played. As I became mindful of my past and the needs of these kindergarteners going forward, I easily increased the quality and quantity of my visits to the kindergarten room. I did not disregard my childhood experiences; instead, I boxed them up into a piece of experience that no longer fit the jig-saw puzzle that a modern kindergarten can be.

The experiences each of us has had as a child forms an important part of our personality. Instead of denying or avoiding this, we would be best served to accept this fact and deal with it by becoming mindful of our past without allowing it to control our future or the future of the children we serve. It is our challenge to reflect upon our past in a manner that allows us understand ourselves better, but we should never allow our experiences to overtake our need to help children form their own perspectives about life in a healthy manner. I think Alfie Kohn best summarizes this challenge to parents and teachers when he said,

> In my experience, what distinguishes truly great parents is their willingness to confront troubling questions about what they have been doing and what was done to them.

3. Be a good role model for your children

Whenever my eleven-year-old grandson comes to Reno, we like to take a walk together in Oxbow Park. One time as we were approaching the park I picked up a beer bottle and threw it in a trash can. As we were leaving the park, Robert saw some gum wrappers on the pavement and quickly picked them up and placed them in his pocket. In both incidences not a word was exchanged.

Modeling is a powerful observational learning tool. In fact, some would say it is the most powerful learning tool that parents and educators have. It is a tool we carry within ourselves everyday of our life. *What we do usually has more impact than what we say.* This was certainly the case with Robert. I could lecture him about the importance of keeping our environment free of trash, but my actions, without any words, carried the message loud and clear.

It is especially important for teachers and parents disciplining a child for misbehavior to have a model of good behavior to refer to. I should warn you, however, that frequently the children will make their own conscious or subconscious reference to *your own behavior.* If your behavior is not consistent with your ideas, do not expect the power of your persuasion to be very strong. On the other hand, if you have a strong relationship with a child and your actions are consistent with your ideas, you have a very good chance of becoming a positive role model in the child's life. This concept is best described by Neil Kurshan (1989) in his book *Raising Your Child to Be a Mensch* when he said,

> Children do not magically learn morality, kindness, and decency any more than they learn math, English or science. They mature into decent and responsible people by emulating adults who are examples and models for them, especially courageous parents with principles and values who stand up for what they believe.

I have to interrupt this "lofty" discussion with some humor. One Thursday my wife had her haircut and her bangs were cut embarrassingly too short (I am told). Anyway, the next Monday two of her third grade students at Mariposa Academy came to school with their bangs cut really short, just like their teacher.

When Rosa left her class in June, there were three girls and two boys who openly proclaimed they wanted to be teachers someday. More important, many of the students in the classroom had come to model the conscientious and determined approach to academic learning and respect for others that their teacher had tried to model all year. These students passed their state tests that year with flying colors, and most of the students who had cut their bangs too short grew them back.

4. Cut yourself some slack and develop a support system

As a parent and as an educator, I have made mistakes. In fact, I will make many additional mistakes as time moves on. The crux of the matter is that humans are not perfect, and we will always make mistakes. The key issue is how we deal with these mistakes. Will we recognize our mistakes or will we ignore them because of our pride? When we understand we have made a mistake, will we try to remedy it or just turn inward and blame ourselves? These are questions that every parent and teacher must answer for themselves.

I believe it is just as important when a mistake is made to not blame others as it is to not blame yourself. Blame gets in the way of problem-solving in a very subtle way because it takes over our thought processes. Let me give you an example:

Recently, I produced an assembly at Mariposa Academy for kindergarten to second grade students focused upon self-control. Halfway through the assembly, I recognized that I had lost most of the kindergarteners. They were squirming on the floor, and of course, five of them had to go to the bathroom. My adjustments did not work, and it turned out it was a bad assembly. Emotions were high for me following the assembly because I was disappointed and embarrassed by the poor student response to the assembly. Part of me wanted to blame the students, but a bigger part of me wanted to blame myself. I went home with a headache, and luckily, I had an understanding wife who helped me process the event. The challenge was to move away from the "blame game" to problem-solving.

I eventually concluded that the curriculum of the assembly was too abstract and time-consuming for our kindergarteners. The next week I presented a shorter, more concrete and interactive presentation to the kindergarteners in their classroom. Boy, was it fun for the kids and me! The problem wasn't the kids; the problem was in my planning. I had failed to plan a lesson that took into account the developmental capabilities of five-year-olds.

Adults with responsibilities for children make hundreds of decisions a day that directly or indirectly influence these children. When a parent asks a child to take out the garbage or a teacher asks a child to take a note to the office, these adults are making impactful decisions. In a very weird way, I have granted myself a 2 percent error rate in my educational career. That is to say, I pardon myself if I make two mistakes in a hundred decisions with a promise to learn and try to fix the error(s) of my ways. When I was a principal, I learned to grant myself four errors a week during Christmas Week because then I was making two hundred decisions a week instead of one hundred decisions. It was a process of giving myself more forgiveness for errors when times were hectic. As I approach seventy and still work in the schools, I recognize my error rate for self-forgiveness must rise until it is obvious that I can no longer function effectively. The bottom line is that we adults, as imperfect human beings, must grant ourselves room for errors without causing self-inflicted pain. Sometimes, we need some *support* to handle our mistakes in a good way.

When a teenager has a fender-bender that leads to parental restriction at home, the story does not end there. Facebook becomes "lit up" with words of support and disbelief from local teenage "friends" in the community. Sometimes, the support might come from international voices across the world. The support is almost spontaneous and it is a powerful sedative for the distraught teenager who will probably not be driving to school for quite a while. Often times, this same level of support is not available to the adult who has imposed the restriction.

A central theme of the book *Tough Love* (1982) is that loving parents and teachers who must respond to the behavior of children can benefit from the support of other adults who are experiencing similar challenges. The emotional support, the exchange of ideas and the friendship that comes with team-parenting or team-teaching is invaluable to many adults. My wife and I took this idea to another level when we joined a Tough Love group in the 1990s. Other parents gave us solace when they told us they faced the same problems. Better yet, their ideas were helpful to us as we organized our plan to better deal with our son. I can easily see how Tough Love group membership in the 1990s can be replaced by Facebook chat groups for parents in 2017. Face-to-face parent meetings are another alternative that can be valuable. The main idea here is that adults need as much support as children when it comes to important decisions in life. The need for support is compounded for single parents because they do not have a spouse to listen to them and help them deal with their parenting issues. Thank goodness my wife was home when I returned from my embarrassing kindergarten assembly!

In the past twenty years, Professional Learning Communities (PLC) have become a common program in most American schools. In the PLC meetings the teachers discuss curriculum, develop assessments and, most important, lend each other support. It is not uncommon in PLC's for teachers to discuss the behavior of a particular student with a focus upon ways the other teachers can help assist the teacher who is struggling to help the student. The PLC is just another example of adults coming together to support one and other as they face the challenges of educating children.

5. Sharpen the Saw (Covey 1989)

Stephen Covey (1989) has eloquently discussed the need for individuals in leadership roles to "Sharpen the Saw" continuously throughout their lives. In fact, Covey heralded this seventh habit of effective leaders by stating that *"it is the habit that makes all others possible"* (Covey 1989). To explain this concept, Covey uses the metaphor of a woodsman spending hours trying to cut a tree with a dull saw. The lesson of the story is, of course, that by keeping ourselves "sharp," we can accomplish more things faster and avoid the frustration that slow progress on any project begets us.

What does the "sharpen the saw" process represent? Covey is referring to the need for individuals to never lose sight of their important need to continuously grow in the four main dimensions of life: spiritual, mental, physical and socio-emotional (Covey 1998). This is a dynamic process that challenges us throughout life. Let us never forget the fact that parents and teachers are true leaders in every sense of the word, and they would do well to pay attention to this Covey seventh habit of effectiveness.

Countless writers, researchers and philosophers have written articles, novels and books attempting to describe what constitutes a healthy individual. It is far beyond the scope of this book to delve very deeply into this discussion, but I do believe Covey's framework of sharpening the saw in four dimension of life has been very meaningful and helpful to me in my life. I can truly say that I feel more "healthy" as an individual when I have a good balance of these four important life dimensions. Reading, exercising, spiritual meditation, appreciating nature, and maintaining strong bonds with family and friends have been focal points on my saw that need continuous sharpening.

Not only should each of us strive to enrich our lives in the four Covey dimensions, we should also learn to respect the interrelatedness of the dimensions and strive for a balance between them. For example, I truly believe that my cancer was partly caused by an imbalance I had within myself when I had a very stressful job fifteen years ago. Mentally and emotionally I was consumed by my job which allowed little energy for family, exercise and spirituality. The result, I believe, was the onset of my first run-in with cancer. There are many inherent dangers for all of us when one life dimension (in my case, the socio-emotional) is overwhelming the other three dimensions.

Educators who are out of balance as individuals may lose their effectiveness as parents and teachers. It is no wonder that a teacher going through a divorce may struggle to be at the top of his/her game in the classroom. The response to this grim situation is not to despair the conditions; rather, it is to rebalance your dimensions. Perhaps more exercise or greater participation in spiritual events such as community service can help counterbalance the deep socio-emotional hurt of the divorce.

Rebalance yourself

> When my emotions are negative, the more I say increases the likelihood that there will be a negative wake, so I need to say less and listen more.
>
> —Susan Scott

We have all heard the flight attendants on airlines warn parents to put the oxygen mask on themselves before they put the mask on their children. This is such a wise statement, and yet, it is also scientific. We know that humans deprived of oxygen do a lousy job at everything because their brain and body are incapable of functioning at full speed. It is more effective to oxygenate your own brain to maintain full capacity than it is to try to help your children when you are half-capacity. This same physiological and psychological principle is just as much a challenge for parents and teachers trying to educate children. The starting point for good parenting and teaching is, of course, a willingness to take care of oneself first. This is the essence of the IO approach.

We have already discussed the necessity to maintain balance in your life over the long term; it is equally important to *maintain balance in your life over the short term*. This concept is best explained by beginning the discussion with an example:

> A third grade student with significant emotional problems is sent to the office for swearing at another student during recess. When the principal says to take a seat in the office, the boy angrily answers, "I hate this school and you suck as a principal." The principal immediately responds to the student by announcing that he is suspended and he will not be seen on the playground for one month.

I have been in this situation as a principal many times. Sometimes I stopped to give myself "oxygen," and other times I did not. The principal in the example cited appeared to react to the misbehavior prior to administering oxygen to himself and failed to develop a purposeful response.

Upon reflection, the one time I did respond to this type of situation similarly to the principal in this example, my emotions overtook my intellect. My blood was curdling from the child's remark, and he was not going to get away with it! I was out of balance: the socioemotional needs I had at the time prevented me from using my mental capabilities to respond in an appropriate manner to the child. *I was temporarily out of balance.* I needed to rebalance myself before I responded to the child. A short walk to the restroom or a quick glance at the Serenity prayer I had near my desk might have been enough to help me recollect myself and respond to the child in a well thought-out, purposeful manner. This was a time when I needed to develop a response that would be helpful to the child and maintain order in the school.

In the history of American families there has probably never been a parent who was temporarily been *out of balance* when responding to the behavior of his or her children! Not so fast—every parent has been out of balance with his or her children on more than one occasion. The challenge to both teachers and parents is, of course, always rebalancing oneself in order to respond to the child's behavior in a purposeful manner. Taking a walk and vowing to listen more to the child can really help.

Far too often, it is our emotional needs that overwhelm the other three dimensions of our life. When we allow this to happen, the results we get are not often positive. The millisecond pause opportunity we have between our emotions and our actions is what distinguishes us as human beings. It is our intellect that separates us from other animals, and we should never forget that fact.

I often recall as an elementary principal taking a walk on the primary playground during recess following difficult adult meetings in the morning. I was applauded by many for providing extra supervision during the frantic recess period; in fact, I was merely rebalancing myself. The cold crisp air, the spirituality of watching six-year-olds play in the sand and the physical exercise were all factors working together to reenergize me for the next challenge waiting in the office. I never disavowed myself from receiving credit for providing extra supervision, however.

The IO approach is such an important concept for parents and teachers to remind themselves of on a day-to-day basis. Am I taking care of myself, so I can do a better job taking care of the kids? The answer to this question has both a long-term and short-term implications. We all are challenged to continually strive to find a balance in our lives that involves the interrelationships between our spiritual, mental, emotional and physical being. At the same time we must ask ourselves in any given situation whether or not the decisions we are making are reflective of healthy deliberations involving all four dimensions of our being—it's quite a roller-coaster ride.

Summary

The major premise of this chapter is the idea that adults do a better job teaching when they are balanced, comfortable with themselves and focused upon their mission as parents and as teachers. Perhaps, the metaphor of putting the oxygen mask on yourself before you try to help your kids is so pertinent to this discussion because it addresses the importance of taking care of yourself in order to be a better educator for your children and students. Parents and teachers who attempt to understand their history as a child, find support from friends, allow themselves to make mistakes, balance themselves, and most importantly, love their children are well on the path to becoming successful parents and teachers.

Pause and reflect

We are so privileged to have the responsibility of helping children to find their voice and set a course in our complicated world. This challenge we assume is hard work but the rewards are incredible—if we take the time to appreciate them. Our beginning task is understanding our own history, our feelings, our well-being and our living examples as the educators of children. Our guiding task is to step back and appreciate the little steps our children make as they grow into thriving young adults capable of understanding others and making good decisions for themselves. Some questions we may wish to ask ourselves are the following:

- Have I taken the time to understand my family background and how it affects me as a parent and as a teacher? Am I willing to put the best interests of the child ahead of my desire to replicate my past?
- Am I taking care of myself physically, spiritually, emotionally, and intellectually? What have I done for myself this week?
- When I make a mistake, am I wasting brain space by blaming myself or others? Parenting and teaching are difficult jobs with no easy paths to follow.
- Who is a member of my support group? Do I have a fellow teacher or parent I can talk with when things are not going well?
- Do I have a *rebalancing* strategy when my emotions overwhelm me? How will I calm myself the next time a child misbehaves?
- Am I taking the time to celebrate the marvels of childhood that occur in my home and classroom every day?

Chapter Seven

Mission Statement

Begin with the end in mind.

— Stephen Covey

All successful organizations, including families, need to be guided by a mission statement. Our country has a Constitution as a mission statement that promotes freedom, national defense, human rights, and the general welfare of its citizens. Starbucks, on the other hand, is guided by the following mission statement:

> Our mission is to inspire and nurture the human spirit: one person, one cup, and one neighborhood at a time.

Our local school district, Washoe County School District, has the following mission statement:

> The Washoe County School District (WCSD) is focused on creating an education system where all students achieve academic success, develop personal and civic responsibility, and achieve career and college readiness for the twenty-first century.

These mission statements are designed to remain steadfast during changing times, and they become the "lens" in which individuals can judge their past actions and contemplate future decisions. They reflect not only the purpose of the organization, but also the values that members of the organization deem to be important. Americans hold individual freedoms and rights to be very sacred in our country, Starbucks staff are taught to value human spirit in their coffee shops and the Washoe County School District values civic responsibility and career/college readiness in their classrooms. True to these mission statements, one would expect that we live in a society that respects human rights, promotes civic responsibilities in our schools and has friendly-spirited coffee houses.

In one family the mother of two teenage boys does all the cooking for the family; in another similar family each member takes a turn cooking meals. What is the difference between these two families? One major difference may be the different perspectives on what the purpose of parenting is: my guess is that the first parent believes that it is her primary job to provide for the health, safety, and sustenance of her family, whereas the second mother is more interested in helping her sons prepare to be independent adults. Neither approach is better than the other, but the real question is whether each mother is aware of the broad purpose of her actions.

It has been my observation that many parents have never taken the time to discuss and reflect upon the purpose of parenting. This lack of a parenting purpose in a family can lead to unpredictability, strife and sometimes chaos. It is like a rudderless sailboat drifting in the ocean without a destination and subject to all the winds and storms that come and go. The problem is compounded in a two parent family when each parent has a different viewpoint about the purpose of parenting. "If you want to buy a candy bar, take a dollar from your piggy bank and walk to the store," says the mother. The father chirps in a statesman-like manner and says, "Relax, I will take him to the store and buy the candy bar."

The parents are angry with one another, and the kid wishes he had never asked for a candy bar.

I suspect this may be a common occurrence in some homes, and it can be avoided by a sincere parental discussion about the purpose of parenting, consensus building, and translating an agreement into parenting actions. For what it is worth, I prefer the mother's approach, but regrettably, I sometimes assumed the posture of the father. My wife and I did have many discussions about this, and we did form a consensus that was less confusing to our sons.

I have a bias about the purpose of parenting that is commonly expressed throughout this book. The theme, "Set the Angel Free," signifies to me that our role as parents is to prepare our children to be independent in life. Michael Popkin (2007) developed the following statement of parenting purpose that totally makes sense to me:

> The purpose of parenting is to protect and prepare children to survive and thrive in the kind of society in which we live in.

This is a statement of purpose that has as much meaning in homes as it does in schools. Throughout this book I will continually lobby for the fact that parents should include helping to create independent adults in their mission statement. Similarly, teachers should be as focused upon personal and civic responsibilities as they are on academic achievement.

Previously, I mentioned that mission statements should include the purpose and *values* of its organization. It is so important that parents take the time to discuss and settle upon the values that are most important for their family organization. This is not an easy task to do and I suspect it is a subject that most premarriage classes spend extra time discussing. It is time well spent for parents and teaching staffs to discuss their individual values and form a consensus about shared values. Once these shared values are determined, they should be included in the family and school mission statements.

My wife and I come from very different backgrounds, but I believe we were able to agree upon some values that have been very important to us: loyalty to family, hard work, respect for others, and service to community. I wish we could say we have been perfect in our commitment to these values, but this is not the case. Nevertheless, most of our actions have been consistent with these values. It is, indeed, most important that parental actions remain true to agreed-upon values if a mission statement is to have any significance. Having a mission statement without living it is like having a Bible in your bookcase but never reading or following it. I am reminded of a powerful quote by Ralph Waldo Emerson:

> What you are shouts so loudly that I cannot hear
> what you say.

Many of us would be wise to ponder Emerson's sage words over and over as we interact with children. Many pundits will say that children learn more from our actions than our words. I suspect that the best course is to live your values and discuss them with the children in your home or classroom. Most parents who have survived the teenage years will tell you that saying the right thing but not doing the right thing will not get past most teenagers who have a keen sense of what hypocrisy is.

I need to add a disclaimer to this discussion. Living and preaching your values does not mean your children will embrace all your values. This is a good thing. Remember, if we are going to "Let the Angel fly', we must recognize they will fly the direction they want to go. The best example of this I can think of comes right from our home.

We raised our sons to be nonviolent. There were no play guns or real guns in our house and we tried to approach conflicts in a peaceful manner. To make a long story short, our older son, Ray, just retired from the Army after a distinguished career that included two tours in Iraq. Clearly, he never really embraced the concept of nonviolence to the same degree we did! The Army was good to Ray and we have no regrets about his decision to join the Army because it was his decision to make. I am happy to report that both of our sons, Ray and Gary, have assumed many of our family values, but equally important, they have added some values to the list that we underplayed.

Mission statements can be formatted in many ways, but I do believe they should be simple and to the point. I have included a basic template below for a parent mission statement:

Parent Mission Statement

I. Our primary role as parents is to_____

_____

_____

II. We agree to *live* and emphasize the following values as much as possible:

    1. _____

    2. _____

    3. _____

    4. _____

    5. _____

3. We understand that this mission statement is dynamic and it will need to be discussed and reviewed frequently.

_____

(Signed) (Signed)

Once parents have developed a mission statement that they agree upon, this mission statement must be "put into play." This means that the parents must refer to the mission statement as they make important decisions affecting their kid's lives. The same course of action should be followed by teaching staffs when they make important decisions involving their students. Furthermore, it is imperative that school staff regularly review their educational practices to make sure these practices are consistent with their school mission.

The right triangle of decision-making

Everyday parents must make hundreds of decisions affecting the children who they are caring for. Some of these decisions are routine, but some of the decisions are not routine, and they require serious thought. It is these serious decisions that I would like to discuss in more detail. Should I allow our fifteen-year-old daughter to take a "pass" on our grandmother visit or should we allow our son to spend the night with his best friend after bringing home a "deficiency notice" in chemistry? These are decisions that take some careful thought. To help with this decision-making, I would like to suggest a mathematical way to look at these important decisions. I will call this approach the "Right Triangle" approach.

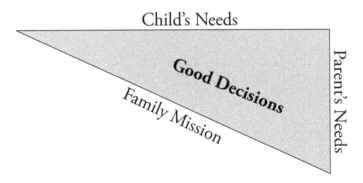

I am not a mathematician, but I do understand a few geometric concepts. I remember that a right triangle has two sides that meet at a ninety-degree angle (perpendicular) and the third side (the hypotenuse) is always the longest side. No matter how long or short the two perpendicular sides are, the hypotenuse will always be the longest side.

I would like to label the triangle in the fashion described below:

- Two ninety-degree (perpendicular) sides: adult needs and child needs
- Long-side (hypotenuse): family mission
- The area within the triangle: good decisions

Using the mathematical properties of the right triangle as I guide, the following rules for family decision-making make sense:

- "Right" decisions are based upon the interplay between three important variables: the child's needs, the adult's needs and the family mission.
- All sides are important and need to be considered when important decisions are made. If one side is neglected, the triangle will collapse.
- The family mission will always be the most important. It is the longest side of the triangle.
- Whenever you increase the importance of the adult's needs or the child's needs, the importance of the family mission will also increase. No matter what the situation, the family mission will always predominate.

It is easy to see that the right-triangle decision-making model can be used in schools as well as in homes. Simply put, the school model would have the two sides of the triangle be "student needs" and "teacher needs," and the hypotenuse would be the "school mission."

It is time to provide an example of the right-triangle decision-making model in practice:

When our younger son was in the seventh grade, he asked us if he could attend a party at a classmate's house. My wife immediately called a few mothers whose teenager sons had also been invited to see if anyone had information about the adult supervision at the home of the party. It turned out that the single parent of the girl throwing the party was known to have alcohol problems. We had a need to know how safe it would be to have our son attend the party. Our son really wanted to go to the party. At the age of thirteen, it would have been his first party, and it represented, in some strange way, a step toward independence and adulthood. The answer to the question was yes, but we did some "behind the stage" maneuvering. One of Rosa's friends, who was in the same predicament, knew the father and volunteered to help at the party. This offer and acceptance by the father allowed us to be confident that our son and the friend's son would be safe at a party that had the potential for young teenage drinking.

In the end, the needs of our son and our needs were addressed, but our mission to keep our son safe prevailed. We recognized that these decisions would become harder as our son matured because our mission to allow him to become independent and his need to become independent would, sooner or later, move the safety issues from our lap to his lap. Nevertheless, the right triangle of decision-making had been a useful guide in our decision-making process for a thirteen-year-old wanting to go to a party.

I should point out the importance of flexible thinking and searching for alternatives when using the Right Triangle approach. It would have been easy to say "No party" to our son based upon our commitment to the "safety" factor in our mission statement; instead, we considered alternatives that would help us make a "right" decision without violating our commitment to our mission as parents.

Chapter summary

Successful organizations "begin with the end in mind." That is to say, these organizations have a purpose and the members under-stand and agree upon the values they must honor on a daily basis to achieve this purpose. School houses and family homes pose no exception to this rule. In this chapter parents have been encouraged to develop a mission statement and follow it. Similarly, school staff have been encouraged to frequently review their decisions using the school mission statement as a reference guide to determine if their actions are aligned with their mission. To assist parents who want to create a mission statement, a template was provided to guide the process and a graphic model was provided to help parents and teachers use their mission statement when important decisions are to be made.

Pause and reflect

- It is important for all parents to create a family mission statement that reflects the purpose of parenting and the values the parents consider to be the most important to live by. Have you taken the time to develop a mission statement and occasionally review it?
- Periodically, parents and teachers need to revisit their mission statement to make sure their actions are aligned with their mission. Have you done this analysis recently?
- The right triangle of decision-making is a helpful tool to use when important decisions are to be made involving the welfare of children at home and in school. Have you tried using this template when important decisions need to be made?
- Memberships in organizations can help individuals to believe in a cause bigger than themselves. Have you taken a moment in recent days to think about how fortunate you are to have a leading role in a family or school organization?

Chapter Eight

Fundamental Principles of Child Discipline

The first seven chapters of this book have focused primarily upon basic parenting and teaching behaviors that help children to strengthen their wings as they prepare to fly into their future. In chapter 8 the focus of the book changes course from the fundamentals of raising children to the fundamentals of child discipline. This change in course makes sense when one broadens the definition of discipline to include all the steps teachers and parents make to guide the behavior of children. Let us never forget that when a parent or teacher chooses a strategy to guide a child's behavior, his or her values, mission, relationship with the child and beliefs are put into play. Child discipline becomes the vehicle for translating the family and school mission statements into action.

The central theme of this chapter is the premise that discipline is a teaching opportunity for adults and a *learning opportunity* for children. This process should be viewed as a challenge, not as a hindrance. In this chapter the basic framework principles of childhood discipline that should govern all disciplinary interactions are discussed. In chapter 9 specific discipline strategies will be discussed in more depth.

When a brother hits his younger sister over a toy, the parents must respond to this behavior. Will the parent ignore the behavior or will the parent take the toy and order both children to their room? Are there other choices to make? Clearly, the parent needs a framework to approach this problem before he/she develops a strategy. The six fundamental concepts that provide a framework for successful child discipline listed below will be emphasized in this chapter:

1. Be proactive: expectations and competency.
2. The goal of child discipline is to help children develop inner discipline.
3. Childhood discipline must be defined as a learning opportunity.
4. Open the parachute: childhood learning occurs when children have an "open" mind.
5. Open the parachute: childhood learning is developmental.
6. Open the parachute: childhood perceptions mean everything.

1. Be proactive: expectations and competency

> The most important step in any disciplinary action is to establish reasonable expectations and boundaries in advance.
> —James Dobson 2014

Do the children in your class understand the rules of the class and the teacher's expectations? If there is a family rule forbidding fighting, do the brothers and sisters in the family know how to solve conflicts peacefully? These two questions highlight the root of many discipline problems in homes and school: clear and reasonable expectations and skill competency. In this section I will discuss both of these very important elements of child discipline. In a true sense, homes and classrooms that have reasonable expectations that have been taught to children and enforced with consistency seldom have major discipline problems.

A. Expectations

I believe that the discussion of adult expectations must be divided into two parts: reasonableness and communication of the expectations. This discussion will begin with the concept of *reasonable* expectations because if an expectation is not reasonable, the communication of this expectation becomes irrelevant. Expectations that are unreasonable doom a child to failure and hard times ahead.

In previous chapters I have discussed the importance of tailoring expectations to be within the reach of a child. This means you would not ask a three-year-old to walk the dog or ask a first grader to take a note to the sixth-grade teacher. As children grow older, the task of discovering what a child should and should not do becomes more challenging to parents and teachers. This is especially true for the parents of children with neurodevelopmental delays. Mel Levine in his excellent book *A Mind at a Time* (2004), addressed the harsh reality of unfair expectations on learning disabled children when he said:

> Some children end up paying an exorbitant price for having the kind of mind they were born with. Through no fault of their own, they are the owners of brains that somehow do not mesh with the demands they come against, requirements like the need to spell accurately, write legibly, read quickly, work efficiently, or recall multiplication facts automatically. When they grow up they will be evaluated on their specialties; in childhood they will be evaluated ruthlessly on how well they do everything.

Dr. Levine's message to all of us is to make a special effort to try to understand the strengths/weaknesses of *all* children in order to formulate reasonable expectations.

I remember taking a family counseling class many years ago from one of my favorite professors, Dr. Jerry Downing, at the University of Nevada Reno. Dr. Downing reminded us over and over that one of the key factors in successful parenting of teenagers was *flexible expectations*. That is to say, if a nine-o'clock curfew was reasonable for a thirteen-year-old, the curfew might need to be expanded to midnight for a seventeen-year-old based upon the teenager's history. I do not think Dr. Downing's message was reserved for teenagers—we must always be willing to adjust expectations as children mature and as we learn more about the strengths/weaknesses of our children.

The *communication and implementation* of expectations is a dynamic process. It happens every day of our lives as we respond to the behavior of children. I believe there are three parts to a good expectation:

1. Discuss the expectation.
2. Teach the expectation.
3. Enforce the expectation.

The best example of this process occurs every August in thousands of classrooms across the country. During the first week of school teachers work with their students to generate classroom rules. Student feedback is solicited and listened to, but it is not always the decisive element because teachers must honor the school mission statement as a priority. Once rules and expectations are decided, the teacher discusses these rules and initiates practice sessions. *There is nothing cuter than first graders walking down the halls practicing "bubbles in their mouths" on the second day of school.* Finally, teachers must boldly enforce the rules when they are violated. Undoubtedly, the quickest way to lose the effect of a rule is to not enforce it. The best way to strengthen a rule is to enforce it AND practice/discuss it throughout the year.

Harry Wong in his wonderful book *The First Days of School* (1991) says, *"Effective teachers MANAGE their classrooms; ineffective teachers DISCIPLINE their classrooms."* He makes a very strong argument that having reasonable rules and expectations that are discussed, practiced and enforced are a cornerstone of well-managed classrooms. Of course, Harry could have rewritten the book with a few changes and entitled it *The First Days in the Home* for new parents—the same principles apply.

B. A question of competence

> Children do what they CAN do.
> —Ross Green, *The Explosive Child* 2014

If a child is constantly fighting on the playground, does this misbehavior occur because he does not want to comply with the rules OR is the misbehavior a result of poor conflict management skills? The answer to this question, of course, guides the next phase of intervention. If the child has experienced poor adult role modeling involving conflict, the long-term resolution of this problem may be providing the child more counseling support to learn conflict management skills. It is far better to prevent misbehavior by teaching a skill than it is to respond to misbehavior over and over with punishment.

I easily remember a time when I suspended a student named Aaron for calling a teacher a "bitch" only to be called an "idiot" by his father when our discipline conference occurred. Aaron's father was not willing to listen to the circumstances of the event and his breath smelled of alcohol at eleven in the day. After the father left, I had deep sorrow and some reservations about my actions. I knew I had needed to respond to the child's misbehavior in a strong manner, but was suspension into the home of a possible alcoholic the best response? When the suspension conference was over, Aaron's father left angrily, the teacher felt justice had been served, Aaron left with a smug smile on his face and, honestly, I did feel like an "idiot."

What does the scenario detailed above have to do with the "competence" question? As I pondered the incident walking around the playground, I really wondered if Aaron knew how to respond to frustration in an appropriate manner. In other words, did he have the skills to respond to the teacher fittingly when she called him out for not doing his homework? After watching his father's inappropriate behavior in my office, I doubted Aaron had ever been exposed to good *modeling* of anger management and frustration tolerance skills.

Could Aaron be following the lead of his dad, his best friend, or is it possible that Aaron's choice of Rap music is laced with people calling authority figures "bitch" over and over? We must never forget that the spheres of modeling influence may begin with the family, but they can extend to extended family, friends and society as a whole (Bronfenbrenner 1979).

I was reminded of a quote that was shared with me by a friend when I became a father for the first time:

> Children have not been very good at listening to
> their elders, but they have never failed to imitate
> them.
> —James Baldwin

We had a job ahead of us! Aaron's behavior, compounded by observations of his father, told us that he lacked skills (competency) to control his anger. The post-incident focus of our school team was to teach Aaron anger management skills and try to reward him when we saw emerging skills appear. On a side-note, we tried to include Aaron's father in this process unsuccessfully, but our counselor and teacher became more vigilant about recognizing possible signs of abuse surrounding Aaron.

One of the first questions I ask myself when a child misbehaves is this: *Does the child know how to behave the right way and does the child have the skills/practice to behave the right way?* This is not an easy question to answer, but the first step in this analysis is usually to review the *modeling* of behavior the student has been exposed to. In Aaron's case, it was easy to see that the modeling of anger management he had been exposed to was not a good one. In other cases, the influence of modeling can be less obvious.

If teachers and parents are going to help children meet accepted behavioral expectations in settings, they must identify the skill deficits these children have. It is certainly easier to identify academic skills deficits in children than it is to identify social skills deficits in the same children. For example, it is less challenging to measure a child's multiplication mastery levels than to measure a child's ability to "accept criticism." Nevertheless, we must endeavor to broadly assess a child's social skills when the child is exhibiting maladaptive behavior as the first step toward teaching new skills. If a social skills deficit is identified, it is up to the school team or parent to develop a plan to teach the adaptive skill that is lacking.

If it is apparent that a child lacks a social skill, the intervention team, including the parent, must develop a plan to help the child learn and practice new behaviors. I really like the teaching model that is put forth in the Boys Town Education Model (Connolly 1995). The BTEM system for *corrective teaching* steps for dealing with misbehavior include the following:

1. Offer initial praise or empathy.
2. Describe the inappropriate behavior.
3. Describe the appropriate behavior.
4. Give a rationale.
5. Practice.

The BTEM model for classroom management painstakingly provides descriptions of "appropriate" behaviors. For example, the skill of "getting the teacher's attention" is broken down into these components:

1. Look at the teacher.
2. Raise your hand.
3. Wait until the teacher says your name.
4. Use a nice voice.

I have seen many teachers and some parents take the time to describe appropriate skills for children in very specific terms similar to the BTEM model because this process can be helpful for some children. One must be careful to recognize that skill training can be a cumbersome process that takes time and much practice. I like Madeline Hunter's conclusions about this process as reported in Harry Wong's book (1991):

> For a child to learn something new, you need to
> repeat it on the average eight times. For a child to
> unlearn an old behavior and replace it with a new
> behavior, you need to repeat the new behavior on
> the average twenty-eight times.

I think Madeline Hunter's commentary is very important because many adults fail to realize how long it takes for a child to learn a new behavior. We are often too prone to give up on a child when he does not demonstrate newly-taught behaviors right away. I am glad my wife has not given up on me as I try to learn to cough on my sleeve and not my hands—I am on my twentieth attempt to remember.

Whenever a child misbehaves, the attending adults must ask themselves whether the child has the background and skills to behave the right way. This is not an easy analysis, but the answer to the question is usually pretty obvious after listening to the child and attempting to understand the child's "world." The second part to this question is establishing what the "right" behavior is and developing a way to teach this skill. I can't begin to tell you how many teachers and parents I have met with who were experts in telling me what a child did wrong, but not so good at telling me what the child should have done right. Lastly, when a team decides to help a misbehaving child learn a new skill, they must build practice and patience into their plan. Neither Rome nor a child can be "rebuilt" in a day.

In summary, it is a common mistake made by parents and teachers to jump quickly to the punishment side of misbehavior before adequately trying to understand the root causes of the misbehavior. Two of the first questions that need to be asked are simply:

1. *Did the child understand the expectation and was the expectation reasonable for the child?*
2. *Did the child have the skills to do what is expected of him/her?*

When these two questions are considered proactively, the need for discipline is greatly reduced.

2. The goal of developing inner discipline

> We claim that an individual is disciplined when he is the master of himself and when he can, as a consequence, control himself when he must follow a rule of life.
>
> —Maria Montessori

Teachers and principals who are good disciplinarians are tough individuals who *command obedience*! Does this image run across your mind when someone says a person is very good with discipline? I would not hesitate to say that most people think this way when they are talking about discipline. I would agree with the "tough" concept, but I would not agree with the emphasis on obedience. My definition of an effective discipline program is very similar to the ideas espoused by Richard Sagor (1996) when he emphasized three characteristics of an effective discipline program:

- The maintenance of order
- The development of internal locus of control
- The promotion (and teaching) of prosocial behaviors

I have to say that many educators and parents tend to emphasize order and social skills, but they fall short on helping children develop an internal locus of control. Said in another way, a major goal of all discipline programs should be to help children develop their own *inner discipline* (Coloroso 2005) on their way to becoming responsible adults.

What does a "responsible adult" mean? There are other authors who have described this term better than I can. I prefer to fall back upon the description of responsibility that Dr. William Glasser used in his famous book *Reality Therapy* (1965):

> Responsibility is defined as the ability to fulfill one's needs and to do so in a way that does not deprive others of the ability to fulfill their needs.

When one looks at discipline as a "learning opportunity" to develop inner discipline, it changes the basic conceptual framework of discipline to be a *"futuristic"* endeavor. Instead of focusing upon the past events that created the need for discipline, the adult administering the discipline is emphasizing teaching inner discipline and improved behavior in the future. This is such a rich concept. I just wish all of us could step back when child misbehavior occurs and think about the opportunity the misbehavior presents to shape the child's future well-being.

Barbara Coloroso (2005) addressed this concept so well when she said,

> If we parents accept that problems are an essential part of life's challenges, rather than reacting to each problem as if something has gone wrong with a universe that's supposed to be perfect, we can demonstrate serenity and confidence in problem solving with our kids.

Oddly enough, this statement by Dr. Coloroso could hardly provide relief to parents and teachers painfully struggling with misbehaving children; on the other hand, it provides a positive framework to begin working on the problems. Misbehavior often creates an ideal teaching opportunity because of the emotion involved and the necessity for important adult-child discussions.

3. Discipline represents a learning opportunity

One should never forget that the word discipline is derived from the biblical term *disciple*. In its original sense, discipline was systematic instruction given to disciples. We now know that the word *discipline* is derived from the Latin word *disciplina*, which means "instruction" (Marshall 2012). It is patently clear to me that if parents and teachers viewed discipline as a *learning opportunity*, kids would be better treated, bad behavior would be easier to change and adults would be happier. It is as simple as that. The next few sections of this chapter focus upon important elements of the discipline learning process that teachers and parents are wise to pay attention to.

4. Open the parachute: childhood learning occurs when children have an "open" mind

> A mind is like a parachute: It only functions when it is open.
>
> —Thomas Dewar

The most important tenet of this section is that the discipline process is a teaching opportunity for adults and a learning opportunity for children. With this idea in mind, the discussion of *how* children learn becomes an important issue. Perhaps the most important shift in educational paradigms that has occurred in my forty-five years career as an educator has been the shift in focus from emphasizing "proper" teaching techniques to emphasizing student learning outcomes. Educational leaders are more impressed nowadays with evidence of student learning than they are with teachers demonstrating good teaching practices. There has never been a greater pressure for teachers to understand *how* students achieve important learning outcomes than there is now—and this is a good thing. The beginning phase of student learning is establishing a *readiness* on the student's part to learn new ideas.

In this section I will discuss important conditions that influence whether or not a child is "ready" to learn. The metaphor of the parachute fits well with this discussion because it certainly illustrates the idea that the mind must be "open" to new ideas if learning is to occur. A child's mind that is inattentive, uninvolved, fearful or over-stimulated seldom learns from the teaching or guidance of an adult. On the other hand, children who are emotionally involved, focused and listening to an adult who is trusted have a great opportunity to learn important lessons. In the paragraphs that follow I will discuss two important factors that often lead to increased readiness to learn: emotion and relationships.

BASIC IDEAS AND STRATEGIES TO HELP PARENTS AND EDUCATORS RAISE SUCCESSFUL CHILDREN WITH INNER DISCIPLINE

A. The importance of emotion and stress

Do you remember your first trip to the principal's office? I sure do. I was in the bathroom when a group of sixth graders blew up cherry bombs in a toilet near me. I was a scared little second grader who ran back to class as fast as I could. Eventually, I was called to the office as a witness but I believe I was too scared to be of any help. I can remember this incident so well but I cannot remember my teacher's name or what stories we read that year. Why is it I can remember the bathroom incident easier than I can remember other important events? You guessed it—it was the emotion that accompanied the incident.

Psychologists have long recognized that emotions affect our learning and, more specifically, our long term memory. John Medina (2008) has reviewed countless studies of the brain and concluded, "*Emotionally charged events persist much longer in our memories and are recalled with greater accuracy than neutral memories.*" Psychology texts often refer to these memorable experiences as "flashbulb memories" that are based upon distinctive episodes in our lives (Feldman, R. S. 2010). We can take advantage of this important concept when we discipline children because the correction of most misbehavior is usually highly emotional.

I can easily tell you that whenever I have been in trouble in life, my emotions have been on high alert. Whether it was a fear of being punished or just a worry about being wrong, I was emotionally involved. I believe the same is true for nearly all of us. The major point here is that the emotionality that accompanies discipline situations provides a *platform* for increased student learning. Could it be that a parent who wants his/her child to learn cooperative skills may have an easier time teaching the child this concept when the child has hit a peer over a toy than beforehand? The key variable in this situation is the willingness of the parent to see the violence and emotion of the situation as, in fact, a time for problem solving and teaching. Let us say, the parachute is usually really open when kids are in trouble and parents and teachers have ample opportunity at these times to turn the situation into a "teachable moment."

There is a caveat to this discussion of emotion. Too much emotion, usually stress, can be a barrier to learning. This fact is also well-researched in psychological circles. In very simplistic terms, we all have a threshold of stress that is good for us, but when we go beyond that threshold, learning diminishes. Goleman (1998) refers to helpful stress as *eustress*, but he carefully reminds us to avoid the debilitating stress that often derails the opportunity to learn from mistakes. Stressed-out children are not good learners.

One of Medina's (2008) brain rules is, "Stressed brains don't learn the same ways." In his discussions of this important topic, Medina points out that children handle stress in very different ways. Some children can be lectured for their wrongdoings in front of the class and others would be totally incapacitated if this happens. There is an important message to all adults disciplining children in this discussion: if you want the child to learn from his/her misdeeds, limit the stress, pay attention to the child's stress reaction, and defuse the situation before you begin the learning cycle.

As a principal I intuitively knew which children I could be "fierce" with and which children I could not be fierce with as I attempted to discuss disciplinary actions. In retrospect, I believe I was merely judging the stress reaction of these children as a factor influencing my approach with them.

Vince Lombardi, the great football coach, often repeated a favorite expression of mine that he tried to follow each day when communicating with his players: *"Praise in public and criticize in private."* He knew that public criticism is very stress-provoking. Perhaps, Vince Lombardi was more of a psychologist than we knew about because he recognized the negative effect of stress. In any case, whether you call it respect or stress reduction, he developed a technique with his players that allowed him to be the great teacher and coach he was. We should all follow Coach Lombardi's lead.

B. Relationships trump substance

Our impact and influence is directly related to our interpersonal relationship with the child.
—Dr. H. Ginott

> You can't make people angry and sell them some-
> thing at the same time.
>
> —Fay and Fay 1995

Who was the most influential teacher you ever had? Some people will respond to this question by mentioning a parent, a teacher
or sometimes a coach. What is most interesting is to listen to the
reasons why individuals picked these people. Predictably, you will
hear comments like,

> She trusted me and encouraged me.
> He made me feel important.
> I always felt supported in my efforts because I
> knew she cared about me.

There is a theme that abounds when you ask people why individuals were such influential teachers or mentors in their life. This
theme is, of course, the positive relationships and emotional attachments that existed between the teacher and the student were critical
to the learning and influence processes.

This emphasis on the importance of emotions and positive relationships in the learning process is not new. Psychologists studying
the human learning process have continually cited the relationship
of emotionality and learning. Perhaps the most influential counselor of my generation, Carl Rogers, posited that effective counselors
attempting to help individuals learn more about themselves must
have an empathetic relationship with counselees that is based upon
unconditional positive regard (Friedman and Schustack 2012). Carl
Rogers and most psychologists would contend that the socio-emotional aspect of learning plays a dominant role in the learning process. John Medina (2008) perhaps best summarized the findings of
many of these famous educators by stating,

> Our ability to learn has deep roots in relationships.

As I began to write this chapter, the stories of three celebrated teachers often bounced in and out of my mind. Each of these teachers recognized the importance of their emotional relationships with each student in their classroom. The three teachers are: Jaime Escalante, Mr. Kotter of "Sweat hog" fame and Harry Wong.

Fifty years ago one of the most popular TV shows on the air was *Welcome Back, Mr. Kotter*. It was a show that humorously presented the efforts of a laid-back teacher trying to motivate and connect with a small group of inner-city students who struggled to find success in traditional classrooms. Mr. Kotter's success with these students was based primarily upon the compassionate but trusting relationship he had with each student. One line from a particular evening show caught my attention as representing Mr. Kotter at his best:

> Mr. Kotter: I am a teacher. That's what it says on my locker, "Mr. Kotter, Teacher." And I am teaching a bunch of students called Sweat hogs. Now, contrary to public opinion, Sweat hogs are not dumb. I mean, a dumb person does not think of a way to make it rain in the gymnasium.

> Vinnie: I did that.

Notice how Mr. Kotter was able to "connect" with Vinnie in a very nontraditional manner. At that point in time, Vinnie's parachute was open, and he was ready to learn. If you want to know how Mr. Kotter orchestrated the next cycle of learning for Vinnie, you will have to watch the show.

During the 1970s a similar inspirational story to *Welcome Back, Mr. Kotter* was taking place in East Los Angeles. This story, memorialized in the movie *Stand and Deliver*, was a true story never to be forgotten by many young educators like myself. It was the story of Jaime Escalante, a Bolivian-born teacher, who struggled to help high school students from poor families pass the AP college exams. In a very persistent manner, Mr. Escalante established *strong bonds* with each student, demonstrated incredibly high expectations and provided effective teaching to all his students. The students did so well on the AP test that the AP Board requested a retesting that did occur with the same results.

Harry Wong has been one of the most celebrated teachers and lecturers of modern times. Mr. Wong is best known for his emphasis upon the teaching and reteaching of classroom procedures as a means to develop good classroom management. His message to teachers went way beyond the emphasis on teaching procedures to include helpful management and teaching strategies. Not unlike many principals, I provided each first year teacher in my school a copy of Harry Wong's famous book, *The First Days of School* (1991).

Mr. Wong greeted all his students each day by first name and tried to connect with his students in unique ways. His comments about student relationships are very profound:

> When you look at the truly effective teachers, you will also find caring, warm, lovable people. Effective teachers know they cannot get a student to learn unless the student knows the teacher cares.

Certainly there are many more stories of successful teachers, parents and coaches who have used their relationship with students to motivate students and open their minds. During my tenure as a principal I observed many teachers who had exceptional discipline and achievement in their classrooms but could not put their finger on why they were so successful. I knew why—the kids had such a strong relationship with the teacher that they did what she said to do, and they listened to her intently. Some of these student actions may have occurred because the students did not want to disappoint their teacher. Just as a positive teacher/student relationship is an important ingredient affecting student learning, a positive parent/child relationship is critical to child development and maturity.

How many parents destroy their relationship with children over homework? As a principal and counselor, the homework issue came across my desk frequently, especially with adolescents. My advice to parents was pretty simple—do not allow the homework issue to sabotage your relationship with the child. The basic theme here is that your relationship with your child must be preserved whenever issues like homework and chores are addressed. Don't worry—there are many techniques available to teachers and parents that address the issues of homework and chores. The key principle here is that a positive relationship opens the parachute for learning and a negative relationship closes the parachute.

I hope I have established the idea that relationships, teaching and learning are all part of the discipline process. Next, it should be clear by now that a prerequisite for student learning is creating the conditions that allow a student to be ready and open to new ideas. The next step is to teach these ideas in a developmentally appropriate manner using time-tested principles of learning.

5. Open the parachute: childhood learning is developmental

I remember walking one crisp morning with my friend Terry and his young dog in a beautiful park by the Truckee River in Reno. It was Sawyer's first walk in the park on a leash and he was a "bit" wild. Every smell, each pinecone and the occasional goose caused a leash pull that clearly took a toll on Terry's shoulder. When we came around a corner, a rather stately teenaged collie pranced by us step by step with his master. I noticed the dog had a choker chain around his neck and I quickly asked Terry why his dog does not have a choker chain. Terry's reply was one of great wisdom: "Sawyer is not ready for a choker chain yet."

Terry's comment probably had many meanings. I believe that he did not want to "limit" the spirited escapades of his puppy so early in his life. Sawyer needed to smell a pinecone and get nipped by a mother goose as part of his learning experiences. Secondly, Terry recognized that Sawyer's undeveloped brain and immature neck muscles may not be able to associate discomfort on his collar with boundaries. Sawyer was not ready to make these connections and forcing the issue could lead to unnecessary anxiety. Terry has proven to be an excellent teacher and a good dog trainer.

How many times have we seen children asked to do things that they are not capable of doing and then punished for failure? This problem is, of course, parent and teacher expectations, not child capabilities. Alfie Kohn (2005) humorously reminds us to keep the ages of children in mind when he imagines the following scenario:

Parent to a toddler who has just made a mistake in the house: Why in the world would you do that? Are you dense?

Child's imagined response: No, I am not dense. I am three.

Most three-year-olds are not ready to read, clean up their room, or understand how another child feels, but they are ready to pick up the toy they just played with. Adults need to adjust their expectations for children to the capabilities of these children. This takes time, reflection, and an understanding that every child is different. Sometimes the principle of *guide stones* becomes relevant when a parent or teacher wants a child to complete a task that may be developmentally challenging to them. You are probably wondering what I am talking about?

The term *guide stones* came to me as I was trail cycling along the Truckee River in Reno. Unexpectedly, a soaking-wet, aged Irish setter ran across the trail with a big stick in his mouth and a determined look on his face. When I asked the dog's owner about the dog and his stick, the owner related a wonderful story to me. He told me that his dog's vision is deteriorating and stick fetching in river current has become very difficult for him. To compensate for this challenge, the dog owner throws guide stones near the stick to help the dog find the target.

As a result of the owner's actions, I was able to witness a very determined dog who had worked hard to capture his stick and had it proudly locked in his jaws. The thought immediately came to me that the concept of guide stones can easily be applied to childhood learning. When we ask children to complete a task that is developmentally challenging, we may often need to throw them guide stones to help them complete the task. The five-year-old who is asked to get ready for school may need a few guide stones along the way. "Let's work on getting your clothes ready first," would be an example of a good guide stone.

There is a very profound message embedded in the concept of recognizing the developmental capabilities of children. This message is the recognition that our responses to childhood misbehavior must be *differentiated* based upon the capabilities and developmental readiness of each child. There are some tasks that children may be capable of doing, but there are other tasks that are simply too difficult or may require different approaches. Similarly, some children are able to understand complex discussions of their behavior and other children are not. Let me provide an example of what I mean:

> Billy and Johnny are two second graders who decide to call their classmate Mary "fatso" at recess. Mary is very hurt by this event and tells the teacher. Mrs. Smith conferences with both boys, but takes a different tact with each boy.
>
> Billy is more mature than his classmates and seems quite perceptive. Mrs. Smith asks Billy to imagine how he would feel if he was Mary and everybody called him "fatso" when the teacher wasn't looking. A good discussion follows.
>
> Johnny, on the other hand, appears to learn things much slower than other students. Recognizing that Johnny does not seem to grasp the concept of understanding others' feelings, she reminds Johnny of his hero, Superman, and asks Johnny if Superman had ever used name-calling to tease people. A good discussion follows.
>
> Both boys miss recess while they develop a sincere written apology to Mary, but the learning approach taken by the teacher was quite different for each boy.

Mrs. Smith is clearly a reflective teacher who responds to student behavior as a learning opportunity that must be adjusted according to student *developmental levels*. She recognized that Johnny was ready to use formal, abstract (Piaget 1972) reasoning at this time in life and Billy was more successful with less abstract reasoning and more "concrete" reasoning.

Good teachers and parents recognize that each child is unique. They understand that children develop physically, cognitively and socially at different rates according to their genetic makeup and lifetime of experiences. Understanding these differences in development is a key factor influencing successful teaching and learning.

John Medina (2008) provided me with a wonderful strategy to remember how children develop cognitively at different rates. He suggested that teachers look at their classroom of students and reflect upon the uneven examples of physical growth (height, weight, puberty) in the classroom and then imagine that the same amount of uneven cognitive growth exists, but is not visible. Taking this analogy one step further, the child who is cognitively "tall and mature" may have an easier time understanding the ramifications of his/her behavior than the child who is cognitively "small" and maturing at a slower rate. The great thing about child development is that most children reach the finish line, but they arrive at different times.

Parents and teachers attempting to teach children and help them learn from their mistakes must pay careful attention to where these children are in the "developmental" track. If discipline, teaching and learning are all considered to be elements of the same process, it is important for all teachers and parents to recognize the uniqueness of each child and the importance of differentiated approaches to learning based upon the developmental capabilities of each child.

6. Open the parachute: childhood perceptions mean everything

I can't tell you how many conferences I had as a principal that began with this statement, "Johnny says that his teacher hates him and Johnny hates coming to school." The usual response to this statement was a defensive statement by the teacher borne out of honest emotions including hurt, dismay and sometimes anger. My role in these discussions was to listen to and support the parent and the teacher and help the newly-created "team" address the specific issues.

One thing I did, however, was to *never trivialize the child's perception* of his teacher or his situation.

It is very clear to me that perceptions are a part of learning that can never be disregarded or underestimated. The truth or falsity of perceptions is secondary to the power they possess over an individual. I will define perception *"as the conclusion we reach as the result of an experience after we have had time to reflect on that experie*nce." (Glenn and Nelsen 1989) These cited authors have reviewed the research about perception and concluded that there are four basic facts about perception that we should understand:

1. *Perception is the key to attitudes, motivation, and behavior.*
2. *Perception is a product of four elements: experience, identification, analysis, and generalization.*
3. *Perception is cumulative.*
4. *Perception is unique.*

I would add to this list the fact that *perception is developmental*. That is to say, one's ability to understand and assess his/her perceptions is directly related to one's cognitive development. A kindergarten student is more influenced by rewards and punishments than he/she is influenced by perceptions; the same might not be the case for a sixth-grader girl capable of abstract reasoning and struggling to see her place in the world. When asked, "Who are you?" the kindergarten student may say, "I am Mary, and I am five," whereas the sixth-grade student may answer the same question by saying, "I am Mary, and I am kind of fat, so the boys don't pay much attention to me." This example demonstrates how perceptions change as our minds develop.

Johnny probably has had a few negative run-ins with the teacher, and his reflections have lead him to believe that the teacher hated him. This conclusion that Johnny has developed could be far from the truth, but it may be influencing Johnny and could be a powerful factor in his life leading to sobbing in the morning and, sometimes, intentional misbehavior. No parent should disregard this sobbing before school and a school conference, no matter how uncomfortable, would be warranted. There is a good chance the teacher may modify her approach to Johnny based upon Johnny's perceptions and Johnny may be assisted to re-examine his perception of the teacher.

It is easy to see that understanding and dealing with childhood perceptions is a fundamental part of the learning process, and it is an essential task adults must face when teaching children. If a child is to learn lessons from disciplinary situations, it is important that we actively listen to the child, understand his perceptions and assist him to evaluate these perceptions. This important process begins with a willingness to listen to the child and value his or her comments. *Effective parents and teachers are good listeners.*

Regardless of what discipline model you use with children, it is important to be a good listener. Sometimes this is hard to do when a student has just called you a "name" in front of three parents in the office. It is something you have to do, however, if you want the child to learn from this experience. When adults *really* listen to children, three important developments occur:

1) The adult can better determine if the misbehavior is a result of competence or compliance factors and what the purpose of the misbehavior was
2) The adult can better understand the issues surrounding the behavior which may lead to better future interventions
3) The child is better prepared to be a problem-solver because the child has had his/her side of the story listened to and emotions recognized.

Good listening involves "getting outside" of your perspective in an effort to understand a child's perspective. I often remind myself that we have two ears and one mouth; in layman terms, this means listen twice as much as you talk. Good listening skills are not easy to define, but most practitioners would agree that the actions listed below are usually displayed by good listeners:

1) *Attend* to the student by keeping eye contact and a supportive body posture.

2) *Show the child you are listening* by paraphrasing and summarizing.
3) *Show empathy* by attempting to identify the child's feelings.

The principles of good listening are best illustrated by the following scenario:

> Pete, an overweight third grade student, was sent to the office from the playground for hitting a student in the back during a soccer game. Anyone passing by him could tell he was about to explode with anger. In fact, the principal, Mr. Smith, was called back to the office because his secretary could tell that Pete was exceedingly angry and close to getting in trouble again. Upon returning to the office, Mr. Smith knelt down (attending) to Pete, and a dialogue began to occur:

MR. SMITH: Pete, why are you in trouble?

PETE: I hit Tom in the back. You don't care. I'll be suspended anyway!

MR. SMITH: You sound really angry (*empathizing*). Tell me what happened.

PETE, *now crying*: Tom calls me fatso whenever I have the ball. This time he tripped me, called me fatso, took the ball, and laughed at me.

MR. SMITH, *summarizing*: Tell me if I have it right. Tom teases you all the time during your games and this time he cheated, hurt you and laughed at you too. You were so mad at him that you hit him?

PETE: That's right!

MR. SMITH: Pete, let's work on these problems so that you can find a solution next time

that won't land you in the principal's
office. I will ask Mrs. Garcia, our counselor, to schedule some time to help you
find a better response to Tom's bullying.
In the meantime, I will be meeting with
Tom after our discussion is over. Okay?
PETE, *in a calmer voice*: Okay.

By listening carefully to Pete, Mr. Smith now is aware that there
are many issues to work through with Pete including: justice for *both*
Pete and Tom, responding to bully behavior effectively and anger
management. Equally important, Pete's willingness to work on issues
has been enhanced because someone listened to him and he has had
an emotional "release." Pete will have consequences for his violence,
but *let the teaching begin.* The first order of business may be to discuss
with Pete how he sees himself relative to his peers. The discussion of
listening to children to understand their perceptions will be revisited
in more depth in subsequent chapters.

Summary

We have learned in this chapter that the key to addressing childhood misbehavior is being proactive with reasonable expectations,
understanding how children learn, and recognizing that discipline
situations can provide teachers and parents the opportunity help
children to expand their learning and change their behaviors in a
positive manner. This concept is one of optimism and hope for the
future because it casts student behavior as a dynamic process that can
be influenced by the adults who the child interacts with often. Child
discipline, in this context, is a process that gives parents and teachers
the opportunity to participate in the child's learning process, and to
help each child to "do well" in a very challenging world by developing inner discipline. The capabilities for success are within the child;
the parents and teachers living with the child can help the child to
unleash these wonderful powers of survival.

The remainder of this chapter reviewed important factors that are involved in childhood learning. Needless to say, there are educational psychology textbooks that delve into this topic in much greater depth than I have. My challenge has been to present the learning concepts that have had the most visible impact upon children during my forty-five years as an educator and as a parent. These abbreviated learning concepts as they apply to child discipline are listed below:

- Recognize that child discipline is a natural opportunity to help children learn more about themselves and to develop lifelong skills for survival in our complex society.
- Children need adult guidance to develop behavioral competencies and understand expectations.
- Pay attention to the emotion of discipline situations and use this emotion as a platform for future learning that "opens" the minds of children.
- Never sacrifice your relationship with a child to make a point.
- Respond to children in a manner that honors their uniqueness and is consistent with their developmental levels.
- Listen to children and pay attention to the perceptions of children—they are real and the source of motivation for future behaviors.

Lastly, one must always keep in mind the destination of the journey this book is written about. I would contend, similar to Maria Montessori and Madeline Hunter, that the primary destination of all child discipline should be helping the child to develop *inner discipline*. If the influential adults surrounding a child succeed in helping the child to develop inner discipline, they have worked themselves out of a job—and it is time to celebrate!

A moment to pause and appreciate

Childhood learning and the development of self-discipline have been the primary focus of this chapter. We should never lose sight of the *miracle* of this learning process and the unbelievable power of children to change their ways in positive directions.

I am often reminded of William Glasser's (1991) plea that *we accept a struggling child "as a person with a wide potential, not just a patient with problems."* In the silent hours of my office I often paused and thought how resounding Dr. Glasser's message was to me, and what wonderful results this type of thinking can bring for children like Aaron and Pete who were experiencing troubles in their lives. Both boys eventually proved that they COULD learn new behaviors and change their lives for the better.

Reflections for teachers

- Do you appreciate and recognize the unique qualities of your students every day?
- Do you make an effort to have a caring relationship with each child?
- Are your classroom rules clear, understandable and reasonable?
- Do you see discipline situations as "teachable moments"?
- Do you teach and model behavior skills and allow students to practice?
- Are you flexible enough to differentiate responses to misbehavior based upon the developmental levels of your students?
- Do you truly listen to students when there is a problem?
- Do you team up with your staff to help misbehaving students change

Reflections for parents

- Do you appreciate and recognize the unique qualities of your child every day?
- Do you make an effort to maintain a caring relationship with your child? Are you paying attention to your child's emotional development?

- Are the family rules and chores reasonable given your child's capabilities?
- Do you teach and model appropriate behavior skills? Are you careful to monitor the behavior models the child sees in his world?
- Do you view discipline in the home as a chore or as a learning opportunity for your child?
- Do you listen to your child and value his or her perceptions?

Reflections for parents and teachers

- Do you appreciate the golden opportunity you have been given to have a positive influence on the life of a child?

Chapter Nine

Discipline Strategies That Work

I remember so well a time when a disgruntled parent confronted me after a parenting class I was teaching and said, "You have taught me the importance of respecting my child and listening to her, but you have not helped me to stop her fighting with her brother!" I never saw her again, but she did make an impression on me. The next week in our class we discussed specific discipline strategies that can be used in homes and in schools. The purpose of this chapter is to outline discipline strategies that I have observed to work with children in a manner that maintains order and fosters *inner discipline.* These strategies are very basic, not new to me, and dependent upon adults following the discipline principles outlined in previous chapters. That is to say, the parent or teacher dealing with the sibling or peer rivalry must empathetically listen to both children, model self-control, attempt to understand each child's perception of events and respond in a reasonable manner that addresses the purpose of the fighting and fosters learning for both children.

The five basic strategies I will discuss in this chapter include the following:

1. The interview—listen to the child
2. Meaningful logical consequences
3. Restorative justice
4. Conferencing for learning

5. Planning for success

1. The interview: listen to the child

There is nothing worse than knowing you are on the just side of an issue, but nobody will listen to you. Children at home and in school need the opportunity to tell their story when they are accused of doing something wrong. The adults listening to the child's story have the opportunity to hear the child's perspective, measure the level of emotion involved, and gather data that helps determine what the purpose of the behavior was. I am a great fan of the "grace and courtesy" concept frequently mentioned by Maria Montessori in her writings. It is extremely important that the adults interviewing children who have misbehaved make every effort to hold off their anger demons and attempt to listen to children with courtesy. This allows the adult to be a better listener, but more importantly, it provides the child with a good example of inner discipline during stressful times.

It is not uncommon for sibling rivalry to occur in homes when big brother and little brother have a fight. Some parents might quickly send both boys to their room for the afternoon without listening to the stories each boy has to tell. It could be that little brother is continuously teasing big brother because he wants him to play with him more often, but this issue will never be addressed by the parent too eager to punish both boys for fighting. In cases such as this family squabble, big issues are often hidden by immediate violence and they appear and reappear going forward. It is up to the adults in these situations to conference, listen and respond to the "deeper" issues" that appear when they actively listen to children.

When I was a first year principal of Lemmon Valley Elementary School, I often had too many children in the office waiting to see me. I felt guilty about the time students had to wait to conference with the principal regarding their misbehavior. Years later, *I do not see wait time for disciplinary interviews as such a bad thing.* It allows students to cool down and think a little about their actions. This idea may have practical applications in homes as well as schools. The idea of a "cooldown period" before the parent or teacher conference with a child makes sense in many cases. This period of time may allow the child to release some of her emotions and tell a story that is more in line with the reality of the situation.

The initial conference that adults have with misbehaving children is a key factor in the discipline process. It is a time to listen to the child, assess the situation and to develop a response to the misbehavior that is fair and meaningful to the child now and in the future. If the adult involved fails to get an accurate picture of the misbehavior, all the following interventions may be unsuccessful.

2. Meaningful logical consequences

> Consequences result in pain coming from the inside;
> Punishment results in pain coming from the outside
> —Fay and Fay (1995)

Two sixth-grade boys, Bill and John, are brought to the principal's office for fighting over a ball on the playground. Because fighting is against school rules and considered to be a serious infraction of the rules, both boys are sent home for the day and assigned Saturday school to learn conflict management skills. As the boys are leaving the school office, each boy has a comment:

1. Bill says, "John should have let me have the ball, and I hate Mr. W. for making us come to school on Saturday."
2. John says, "I screwed up. We could have found a way to share the ball."

There is no doubt that John is on his way to achieving a good measure of inner discipline, whereas Bill is stuck in a pattern of blaming. What has happened in John's life to help him approach his misbehavior in a constructive way? There is no doubt that John's parents and teachers have probably approached disciplinary issues as opportunities to learn and have had good conversations with John about his behavior. Another factor influencing John may be that the influential adults in his life have applied *logical consequences* in situations when John has misbehaved.

Let us never forget that the Skinnerian concept that the consequences that follow a behavior strongly influence the chances that the behavior will occur again. This being the case, how the most important adults in a child's world respond to a misbehavior is a crucial factor determining whether or not the behavior will be repeated. It is my opinion that the effective use of logical consequences by adults in response to child misbehavior offer leads to improved behavior in the long run. Logical consequences to misbehavior are usually consequences that are not enjoyed by the child but are directly related to the behavior of the child. Some examples of logical consequences (LC) are listed below:

- A child does not do his homework. LC: Do homework during recess or after school.
- A child hits a friend playing football at recess. LC: Restricted playground with no football until conflict management class completed.
- A child cuts a class. LC: Saturday school makeup time.
- A child misbehaves in the store. LC: Not allowed on next family outing due to trust issue.
- A child talks back to a teacher. LC: In-office suspension until an essay about respect and an apology are completed. Stay in the back office until the teacher is free to discuss the incident.
- A child throws rocks. LC: Help pick up rocks from the backyard or playground.
- A child litters in the cafeteria. LC: Lunchroom cleanup duty.
- A teenager fails to complete his chores. LC: No cell phone or tab for (two) days because use of technology contributed to the problem.

The "Cadillac" model of implementing logical consequences occurs when the parent or teacher is creative enough to offer two *choices of logical consequences* for the child to choose from. This is, of course, a good technique because providing choices to children is empowering. My problem with this strategy is that is hard to do because often adults are "stretched" pretty far just to develop one creative logical consequence.

Pay special attention to the fact that all these consequences are aimed at the child's behavior…not the child. This is such an important focus in most books written about child discipline. By focusing upon the child's behavior, the adults have a better chance of having a good discussion with the child because they are not attacking the child. For example, the child who fails to complete his homework is not spanked for being "lazy; instead, he is mad at himself sitting in his classroom doing homework while others are having fun playing football. This is a mind-set that promotes good discussions and a pathway to inner discipline. There are two elements to consider when applying logical consequences that I would like to discuss in more depth: (a) act, don't yak and (b) meaningful logical consequences.

A. Act, don't yak

Many parents and teachers who have worked with children who have ADHD are familiar with the phrase "Act, don't yak," because they may have read the excellent book by Dr. Thomas W. Phelan titled, *1-2-3-Magic* (2014). In his book Dr. Phelan urges parents to listen to their children when they tell their story, but to ACT without verbal debate once the story is complete. He reminds adults that children are not "little adults" and provides this warning:

> Adults who believe in the Little Adult Assumption are going to rely heavily on words and reasons in trying to change the behavior of young kids. And words and reasons are going to be miserable failures much of the time.

DOUG WHITENER

Dr. Phelan is so right! All one has to do is go to the local grocery store to hear parents lecturing, warning and trying to reason with their children as they go down the aisles with uncooperative children. Dr. Phelan would suggest that these same parents establish reasonable expectations for store behavior, give the children nonverbal warnings and leave the store with the children when the warnings are not heeded. The children may need considerable time in their room (LC) at home to give their mother time to relax from the stress at the store they caused and to develop a plan for better behavior on the next shopping trip. The discussion of the misbehavior will occur later when both the mother and children are open to reason. Dr. Phelan is even more pronounced about his call for action instead of words when he makes recommendations to the parents of teenagers in his book *Surviving Your Adolescents* (1998). In this book Dr. Phelan warns parents against the "four cardinal sins: spontaneous problem discussions, nagging, insight transplants, and arguing." Dr. Phelan is not at all opposed to the post-incident learning discussions between parent and child that are so important; instead, *he warns against too much discussion* during the administration of consequences.

I believe we can learn a lot from Dr. Phelan about managing the behavior of *all* children. This is certainly true in home environments and equally true in classrooms. Ask any principal what factors distinguish a teacher with good management techniques from a weak teacher, and you will certainly hear comments about "quiet" consequences instead of lectures and warnings.

B. Logical consequences must have meaning

I remember one day talking to a student sitting in our front office who had been kicked out of his classroom for the third time in two weeks. After some time, he confided with me that he would rather be in the front office because it was more "fun" than being in his classroom where he was failing. Ouch! It occurred to me that his teacher might be failing him and we, in the office, might be failing the teacher!

114

Logical consequences, quite simply, must have *meaning to the child*. They are consequences that are not enjoyed by the child and will influence the child to change his or her behaviors. In the case of the office referral child above, the trip to the office brought relief to the child instead of discomfort and some enjoyment watching the office activities. It was now up to me to discuss the child with his teacher to find out what could be done to make the classroom environment more successful and rewarding for this child. Secondly, I met with the office staff to make sure children sent to the office sat quietly in the back of the office away from the entertaining office activities. At our next staff meeting we discussed the difficulties with office referrals and determined that class-to-class time-outs may be more meaningful to disruptive students.

The "in-school" office suspension we were implementing was not working because the time spent in the office was too enjoyable for the students who had been sent there. Now, I would like to give you an example of a "home suspension "system that did work at Delta High in Alaska because the suspensions did have meaning to the students:

> We had a foster home near our high school for students who had displayed behavior problems in other foster homes. The foster parents were strict, caring and consistent. When one of their boys was suspended at school for misbehavior, meaningful consequences were applied at home. Most homes in Alaska have a woodpile next to their home with wood ready to be split for the earth stoves. At this particular foster home, the logs in the woodpile were split by students sent home from school on suspension. Once students in the home recognized the consequences for school suspensions at home, the behavior leading to suspensions ceased!

One of the reasons "home suspensions" do not work very well for many children nowadays is the fact that the parents control the "meaning" of the suspension. If both parents are at work and the student is free to play video games, future behavior change may not occur. Unfortunately, these types of suspensions do not provide meaningful logical consequences to the video-playing children. If, on the other hand, the suspended student is splitting wood all day, different results may be expected.

It is very difficult for parents and teachers to determine whether or not a logical consequence will be meaningful to a child. One rule of thumb I always used was to pose the question, "Is this consequence working?" Clearly, if the teacher constantly sending students to the office had asked herself this question about office referrals as a logical consequence, her answer would have had to have been, "No, it's not working." When a logical consequence is not working, it is time to do some analysis, review the purpose of the misbehavior, and develop a new meaningful logical consequence. During my first session of Saturday School at Lemmon Valley Elementary school I had to undertake this type of analysis:

> I had four third graders who had been in a fight attend the first ever Saturday school at Lemmon Valley ES. From nine to twelve we painted the hallway in the corridor of our sixth-grade modular.

> I thought the event was a great success until one of the boys asked me as he was leaving, "Mr. W., can I come back to Saturday school next week?"

> Clearly, I thought the community service would bother the boys; instead, they enjoyed it. This incident may have provided a testimony to the goodwill all children have inside themselves, but it was probably a consequence that was not going to change their fighting behaviors. The next

> Saturday school was divided into three parts: (1) one hour of sitting with no talking, (2) one hour of quiet reading, and (3) one hour of writing about how the participants would improve their behavior. Believe me, nobody ever asked me again if they could voluntarily attend Saturday school!

The bottom line is that the logical consequence must really matter to the child who has misbehaved. A good case can be made nowadays that school suspensions, parent/teacher lectures and warnings have lost their significance to children.

You may have heard of the term *natural consequences* in your readings. These consequences occur without much adult intervention. For example, if your child forgets his jacket, you allow him to get cold. The job of adults in these cases is simply not to interfere because the child will learn from his cold experience to better prepare next time before going outside. There are limits on the use of natural consequences because children can be hurt. You certainly would not allow your child to suffer the consequences of playing in the street. The bottom line is that sometimes natural consequences can be helpful learning experiences for children, but safety has to be an important concern.

What about punishment? We have all been punished and many of us believe it can be a very helpful intervention with children. Let's look at punishment a bit more carefully, however. I have no doubt that punishments such as a spanking create obedience but they do not create *responsible thinking* (Marshall M. 2012). In fact, the child who is spanked for stealing can feel good that his or her consequence is quick and relatively thoughtless. This child has been spared the agony of parental discussion, apologies, restitution and other measures that may cause the child to have long-term doubts about his own behavior.

There is a dangerous element to many punishment strategies used by adults attempting to correct the behavior of children. The danger is the fact that poor adult modeling of anger control often overtakes the adult message. That is to say, the child consciously or unconsciously responds more to the adult example of poor anger control than to the message about his or her behavior. In fact, James Dobson, author of the *Strong-Willed Child* (2014), has noted that the most common error in disciplining children is the inappropriate use of anger to control children. Punishment and anger tend to go hand in hand, and they are a dangerous combination for children.

I am not an advocate for corporal punishment, but I have to say I did see spanking used the proper way when I was a counselor in Alaska:

> Our principal, Ron Beck, was a very kind and thoughtful man who did a good job understanding children. When a young child under the age of ten committed an act that was serious, the child was spanked with a witness (usually me) present. Ron made sure five factors were in play when he spanked a child: (1) the misbehavior was severe, (2) the child knew why he was being punished, (3) Ron was totally calm, (4) the child had a postpunishment conference with the counselor to discuss improved behavior, and (5) follow-up occurred. Unbeknownst to most staff, Ron disliked this task and usually invited me afterward into his office to have a cup of coffee and settle himself.

If all corporal punishment was administered using Ron's guidelines, it might be considered an acceptable intervention. The truth of the matter, however, is that states have banned corporal punishment in schools because, done improperly without good guidelines, it can be abusive and dangerous. The same reasoning can easily be applied to the use of corporal punishment in homes.

3. Restorative justice

> When we rely on rules rather than relationships
> when harm's been done, we all lose.
> —Amstutz and Mullet 2014

Many times the misdeeds of children and adults cause harm to other individuals. In these cases, typical logical consequences are necessary but not sufficient. It is important that some form of *restitution* (compensating for harm) be applied.

The concept of restitution as a logical consequence to misbehavior is deeply embedded in our system of justice. Most crimes have a victim and a civil action for damages. OJ Simpson may not have been convicted of a capital crime, but he most certainly had to pay restitution to the Goldman family. I like the idea of restitution as a response to misbehavior for many reasons:

- It is a fair system that is consistent with the laws of our society and very logical.
- The victim of the behavior does get some form of relief and has the opportunity to practice forgiveness.
- The form of restitution causes the child to think more about his or her actions. The child has a better chance of capturing the event in his or her long-term memory and learning a valuable lesson.
- Restitution is a negative consequence that will frequently limit the misbehavior from occurring again and does not carry with it the secondary learning that direct punishment (e.g., spanking) may cause.

I would like to take the action of restitution one step further. I truly believe that in schools and in homes restitution is important, but often not sufficient. It is important to respond to the harm others have suffered in a meaningful way that can *lead to repaired relationships in the future*. This process of restitution (compensating for harm) and trying to improve relationships will be referred to as *restorative justice* (RJ) in this chapter of the book.

I have to say that I especially like the focus upon the future and repairing relationships in the RJ approach because a child who has harmed another child will see their victim in the classroom the next day or the next hour. If this child can learn to understand and accept responsibility for the harm he has caused and step forward to mend relationships, what a powerful life message has been taught! Restitution alone is a good consequence for behavior that has harmed others; restorative justice (RJ), on the other hand, is a better intervention because it involves a focus upon *relationships* as well as compensation.

I especially like the commentary about RJ that L. S. Amstutz and Judy Mullet provide in their book, *Restorative Discipline for Schools* (Amstutz and Mullet 2014). These authors state that restorative justice

- recognizes the purposes of misbehavior,
- addresses the needs of those harmed,
- works to put right the harm,
- aims to improve the future,
- seeks to heal, and
- uses collaborative processes.

This RJ concept is best illustrated by an example of RJ that I experienced in my life:

When I was in the third grade, I remember stealing a candy bar from a store in my neighborhood and getting caught. How my parents knew I had stolen the big Mounds bar in my pocket, will never be known by me—they just knew. I did get a spanking, but I also had to apologize to the store manager and clean his front sidewalk. Needless to say, I remember the agony of the apology and the sidewalk job better than the spanking. It did turn out that the store manager was an understanding man, and he gave me a candy bar on the day I cleaned his sidewalk. The event is permanently on hold in my long-term memory. I cannot remember ever stealing again except for an occasional Motel 6 hand cloth. Restitution, the act of compensating someone for damages, was an important part of the consequences for my action. More important, I had learned to face my victim, ask for forgiveness and do what I could do to save our relationship. It would have been easier if I had JUST BEEN SPANKED!

The most common form of RJ I used as a principal was the apology. Done in the right manner with good expressions of remorse, the apology can be a very effective tool to repair relationships, especially with young children. I can't tell you how many times I have seen young children spontaneously hug each other after a heart-felt apology. Sometimes the apology is a sufficient intervention to address minor misbehavior, but other times the apology is only one part of the intervention. I recall a quote by Ed Orszulak in his book the *Redemption Approach* (2007) that stuck with me in my last few years as a principal:

> The act of forgiveness is a process of absolution; however, forgiveness does not imply an absence of accountability. Forgiveness simply fills part of the void left in a relationship from one act of disturbing behavior. Restitution, an act of rebuilding and repairing, continues to fill the void.

As a principal, I agreed with Mr. Orszulak's stance on apologies and usually the apology was accompanied by a consequence that often involved another form of restitution to the victim. One has to remember that RJ is focused not only upon restitution, but also the concept of repairing relationships. Not once, but many times, name-callers on our playground were required not only to apologize to their victims, but they were given the additional job of protecting the victim from other name-callers on the playground. This would be a good example of a secondary form of restitution designed to improve relationships.

One has to be a bit careful with the apology concept. In my limited review of "bully" research I have seen a definite pattern of avoiding face-to-face meetings between the bully and the victim because this is intimidating to the victims and the apologies are often hollow. Once again, an apology must be heartfelt in order to have meaning.

The form of the apology can be developed in many ways. I believe it is important that the child be asked to

1. explain what he/she did wrong,
2. discuss the problems that would be created if other people did the same thing,
3. explain what he/she will do *differently* the next time, and
4. apologize and ask the victim if he/she will *accept* the apology.

There is considerable discussion and practice before the formal apology occurs. In most cases, the child is asked to role-play the apology with me prior to completing the apology with the victim. This is the time when the adult involved becomes a teacher and the child becomes a learner. The Boys Town protocol for apologies (Connolly 2007) has greatly influenced my practices and it is a good model to use.

It has been mentioned previously that the consequence "must fit the crime." This being the case, frequently a more creative form of RJ is called for. The best way for me to address this subject is to provide two memorable examples of RJ from my career as a principal:

1. One afternoon I was a bit shocked to hear that four boys on our playground were shouting out racial slurs in the direction of an elderly Asian neighbor two houses away from our Peavine School playground who was painting her fence. After investigating the event I learned that what had been reported to me was, in fact, the case. My passion for racial tolerance overwhelmed me with anger as I learned about this case, but I managed to stay calm as I told myself over and over that I was the adult and this was a learning opportunity for these boys. After considerable thought and

group discussion, I assigned the boys the tasks of apologizing to the woman and serving detention after school painting the woman's fence.

All of the boys' parents were "on board" with this form of restitution except one parent whose son was allowed to serve an alternate detention. The boys finished painting the fence and received the ultimate gift from the lady in appreciation: Chinese egg rolls. I do believe that the three boys learned a valuable lesson about racism and relationships, especially when the neighbor brought the boys those egg rolls.

2. Sometimes principals get disturbing calls from parents early in the morning regarding events that happened the previous day. More often than not, the "facts" reported by the child at the dinner table are exaggerated or a bit fabricated, but follow-up is necessary. On this one occasion on a Friday morning the facts were only somewhat consistent with the report.

A little first grader had come home without eating lunch, and she had tattoos on her arms. She reported that older students had forcibly drawn tattoos on her arms and taken her lunch money. After spending a considerable time investigating this report from an incensed mother who was ready to pull her child from our school, I learned that three of our Peavine third grade students had a tattoo enterprise on our campus during morning recess. They were selling tattoo artistry for fifty cents to first graders. It turned out that our playground was full of first graders with tattoos and comparatively rich third grade girls. How was I going to handle this?

The third grade girls were invited to spend "Saturday school" with me. During the two-hour period, the girls were read a story about helping others, and we discussed the concept of older students being fair and not taking advantage of younger children. The girls wrote apologies to the first graders and each girl drew a tattoo picture to be given to her "tattoo victim" in my office the next Monday.

Lastly, I did want to honor the enterprising spirit of the girls. We spent some time brainstorming ways they could make money without taking advantage of people. It would be fun to replay this Saturday school scene with a group of Wall Street corporate leaders.

In many situations the victim of misbehavior is a *community* as opposed to an individual. The victim of the child who throws rocks on the playground is the school community because the playground is no longer safe. In these cases, restitution goes to the community, not individuals. The child who threw rocks must spend a few recesses picking up rocks to make the playground safer. This intervention is so parallel with the actions of our local community adult courts and "community service" sentencing.

Parents and educators must have the proverbial "bag of tricks" in hand if they wish to turn disciplinary actions into learning opportunities. The use of RJ as a logical consequence should never be overlooked when taking disciplinary action with a child. RJ as an intervention provides the opportunity for fairness, relationship building and forgiveness in a world that is often too focused upon punishment as an end in itself.

4. Conferencing for learning

Learn to listen to your child heart to heart and then respond with knowledge and empathy and you will reach her at a level that creates the tie that tames.

—Michael Popkin 2007

The postdiscipline conference may be the most important step in the disciplinary process. It is the time when well-meaning adults make an extra effort to help the misbehaving child *learn from his experiences*. It is a time when the communication of love and respect are of the utmost importance.

The postdiscipline conference should occur when the child has settled down and is ready to learn. This is a time when the parent or teacher must make every effort to be an active listener. *It is a time when the focus has to be on helping the child to develop inner discipline.* Asking thoughtful questions of the child will always advance the cause of inner discipline much quicker than lecturing or preaching the gospel of your own experiences growing up. Some questions that I am particularly fond of are:

- Did your behavior work for you?
- If everybody did what you did, how would things be at our school (or in our home)?
- How do you think your friend felt when you did/said this to him?
- What would the person you respect most in class have done in this situation?
- What will you do differently next time that may better help you meet your needs?
- What lesson have you learned from this event?
- How will this event make you a better person?

As a principal I tried to walk through classrooms on a daily basis. During these brief visits to classrooms, I looked for many indicators of good teaching and student learning. One indicator that I always appreciated was teachers taking a brief moment to conference individually with students. Sometimes these conferences clearly were focused upon academics, but other times these conferences were centered upon behavior using the aforementioned questioning strategies. Without exception, good teachers find a way to do this conferencing and it is so important!

When a parent or teacher takes the time to conference with a student following a misbehavior event, it is a powerful moment. This adult is conveying to the child a message that none of us is perfect, and we care about the future of the child. Done properly, this conference is also a time of respect because the *adult leans on the child to find the error of his ways and assists the child to construct a new pathway of behavior going forward. In essence, this is what the development of inner discipline is all about.*

5. Planning for success

There are many disciplinary situations in which a new plan for success is easy to create. The child understands what he did wrong, meaningful logical consequences have been applied and the child has carefully thought about what he did that was inappropriate. The new plan for success is simply to agree upon the adaptive behavior(s) to be learned and to practice these behaviors by role-playing with the child. Encouragement and follow-up by parents and teachers increase the chances of success for the child.

Alas, parenting and teaching are usually not so simple. There are times when the behavior of a child repeats itself enough that it is clear to see that an unhealthy pattern has been established. This is not uncommon in schools and homes, and it is a challenge that can be dealt with. The first step is for the adults who care for the child to recognize the pattern of misbehavior is occurring that is not helpful to the child. The next step in this process is for these same adults to cease complaining about the child's behavior and to begin brainstorming ideas as a team that may help the child to change his or her behavior. Once it has been established that a child is displaying unhealthy behaviors, it is time for the important adults in the child's life to work together to (1) gather data/information about the child's behaviors and (2) develop a plan that helps the child to learn and practice new adaptive behaviors that work better for the child.

A. Gathering information

Have you ever noticed that doctors have a whole litany of questions that they ask you whenever you go to their office complaining of sickness? The answers to these questions combined with thermometer readings and other tests may determine whether you are placed on antibiotics, sent to the hospital or sent home with some aspirin and ginger ale. These doctors spend extra time gathering information before they are prepared to design an intervention. This is the case because doctors know the intervention must be well-matched with the symptoms presented in order to be effective. This information gathering process is remarkably the same for adults attempting to help a child change his/her behavior. Instead of using a thermometer, I would suggest that parents and teachers use, at a minimum, the five questions listed below to gather information about a child's misbehavior:

1. What is the misbehavior? How often is the behavior occurring? When?
2. How is the behavior hurting the child and others?
3. What are the antecedents (triggers) for the behavior?
4. What are the consequences to the behavior?
5. What is the purpose of the behavior?

This process may seem complicated, but it is not. Let me give you one example of this information gathering process that occurred at Peavine School but also occurs on school campuses on a daily basis:

> A first grade girl, Alice, goes home and tells her father that she is being bullied by Mary. The next day Alice's parents are at the school demanding that something be done about the bullying at school. The principal and Alice's teacher begin an information gathering process by interviewing Alice and checking with the duty teachers.

127

Upon review, it is learned that the behavior occurring is better defined as name-calling by Mary, and it is happening often during first recess when Nancy is on the playground with Alice and Mary. The trigger is the timing when all three girls are together as a three-some on the playground. Both Mary and Alice want the full attention of Nancy, and Mary has learned that if she calls Alice a name, Alice will sulk and go cry under a tree (consequence). This departure by Alice allows Mary the opportunity to play with Nancy alone (purpose).

It is easy to see that the additional information gathered by the principal and teacher will lead to a more effective intervention to stop the name-calling. Although Mary will have some logical consequences, the focus of the intervention will be on friendship skills and how to handle "triangle" relationships on the playground. These three first graders will have an opportunity to learn at an early age ways to handle triangle relationships—a skill most adults struggle with throughout their lives.

B. Plan development

After using thoughtful questions to gather data/information about a child's misbehavior, the most important task facing teachers and parents is to develop a forward-looking plan designed to help the child change his/her behavior. The template I like to use for basic school and home interventions is what I call an "abbreviated PTR" (prevent, teach, reinforce) model patterned after the PTR model pioneered by Dunlap, Iovannone, Kincaid, Wilson, Christiansen, Strain, and English (2018). The most attractive part of this model is the logic behind the model: form a hypothesis about the purpose of the behavior, define the unacceptable behaviors, choose appropriate behaviors that can work better for the child, teach the new behaviors, pay careful attention to the antecedents and consequences that support both behaviors and, finally, take actions to shape the child's environment in a manner that prevents future misbehavior from occurring.

It is important to point out that when I use the term "abbreviated PTR," I am recommending a system that has less rigorous data collection procedures than can be used by parents and teachers on a routine basis. I am a devotee of the PTR logic, and I believe this logic can guide parents and teachers when they see children displaying misbehavior patterns in their settings. Abbreviated PTRs with less sophistication than formal PTRs can be very beneficial to children with behavior problems in homes and classrooms if they are done correctly.

What does an abbreviated PTR process look like? The group of adults studying a child's behavior attempt to gather enough data/information to answer the following questions:

1. What is the misbehavior and how does it affect the child and others?
2. What is the function/purpose of this behavior for the child? This topic will be discussed more thoroughly in the next chapter
3. What would be a more appropriate behavior for the child to learn that will meet his/her needs and not infringe on others?
4. How will "we" teach the child this new behavior?
5. How will we reward the child when he/she displays the new behavior?
6. How will we change the child's environment to prevent future behavior problems?

Once the adult team completes the PTR review, a plan is developed that includes the following components:

1. A description of the new adaptive behavior to be learned.
2. An explanation of how this adaptive behavior will be taught and rewarded.

3. A "prevention" plan that shapes the environment to increase the chances of the adaptive behavior occurring.
4. A follow-up plan that monitors the success of the new plan.

It is important that the new adaptive behavior is simple and something the child is capable of doing. Equally important, the teaching strategies (role-playing, observing others, stories, etc.) must be designed to fit the learning style of the child. If you are interested in learning more about the PTR method, I would recommend you buy the book, *Prevent, Teach, Reinforce: The School-Based Model of Individualized Positive Behavior Support* (Dunlap et al. 2018).

Let's journey back in time to the story of Alice, Mary and Nancy. Clearly, the purpose of Mary's name-calling behavior was to rid herself of Alice, so she could play with Nancy alone. The antecedent conditions were in play when the girls were together at recess; the consequences of Mary's name-calling were positive because Alice sulked and Mary was able to play with Nancy alone. The principal, teacher and probably Mary's mother could react to this situation in many ways, but I suspect an abbreviated PTR might lead to the following plan:

- Mary apologizes to Alice and is not allowed to attend morning recess until she completes a picture of herself being nice to Alice as a gift.
- Mary, Alice and Nancy work with the counselor to create agreements about how they can play together peacefully. Role-playing to practice new agreements occurs.
- Mary receives guidance from the counselor and her mother regarding friendship skills and respect.
- Alice is taught new ways to respond to name-calling by her parent and the guidance counselor.
- Mary is praised by her teacher and parent when she demonstrates defined respectful behavior to others.
- The teacher goes out of her way to help find another friend for Mary to play with on the playground (prevention). This action may reduce Mary's need to always play with Nancy.

I am happy to report that Alice, Mary, and Nancy found betters ways to play together after this incident of misbehavior had been addressed. More important, each girl had learned some valuable lessons about friendships. The principal, teacher and parents collaborated well together using PTR logic to turn a display of misbehavior into a learning opportunity for three cheerful first graders.

Chapter summary

In this chapter some practical suggestions have been offered to help parents and teachers deal with everyday discipline problems that naturally occur as children learn to balance and regulate their needs with the needs of others. Although each disciplinary encounter is different, the author urges parents and teachers to approach each situation with good listening skills, a desire to understand the underlying issues behind the misbehavior and an emphasis on the *goal to help children to learn and practice inner discipline.*

A central theme of this chapter is the idea that children are best served when their parents and teachers focus upon the misbehavior of a child and not upon the character of the child. When the adults who are responding to misbehavior apply meaningful consequences that are logically related to the behavior of the child, there is a natural tendency for the child to rethink his or her behavior instead of blaming others. *This type of behavior-based thinking is the precursor to the development of inner discipline.*

Many times in life the misbehavior of children infringes on the rights of others. In these cases restorative justice is a powerful logical consequence for children because it causes the child to think about the impact of his behavior on others, and it creates the opportunity for relationships to be repaired. The simplest form of restorative justice is the apology, but it can also be described in some cases as the most powerful example of restorative justice when executed with sincere remorse.

It is very important that the teachers and parents who administer logical consequences do a fair investigation of the misbehavior incident, listen carefully and apply meaningful consequences in a calm manner without allowing debate, warnings, lectures or too much discussion. The consequences must have meaning to the child and they must be reasonable.

The VERY important postdiscipline discussion should occur later after the child has had time to calm down. The entire focus of this conference should be on the broad issues that arise during discussions with the child and the selection of a more adaptive behavior to be used the next time a similar incident occurs. This is a time when parents and teachers are advised to remember that their communication with the child needs to be underpinned by an attitude of caring and respect. One could say that the postdisciplinary conference is one of the most critical experiences that a parent or teacher can have with a child because of the intense learning opportunities these situations provide for the child.

When a child is displaying *patterns* of misbehavior, it is time for a team of adults to gather data about the child's behavior and to analyze this behavior. In this chapter the abbreviated PTR was introduced as a systematic approach to behavior analysis that focuses upon the purpose of misbehavior and the development of adaptive behaviors to replace the maladaptive behaviors of a child. The PTR system has helped thousands of children improve their school behavior across the country, and applied the right way, it can be just as effective in homes. One key element of successful PTR programs has always been the unbridled belief by the adults involved that children can be guided to change their behavior in positive directions.

Pause and reflect

How do we get children who have behaved inappropriately to admit that they messed up, accept consequences, and display resolve to do better the next time? There is no easy answer to this question, but the author believes that mature adults who calmly respond to misbehavior by listening to a child, applying meaningful logical consequences and taking the time to conference with a child about behavior choices in the future can, in fact, influence the child to develop *inner discipline*. This is an adult endeavor well worth the time and effort because it helps the child to develop an upward flight pattern. Some questions parents and teachers may wish to think about include:

- Do I do a good job listening to children when they misbehave?
- Is the goal of helping children develop inner discipline in the forefront when I respond to misbehavior?
- Do I respond to misbehavior with meaningful logical consequences? Are these consequences working because they have meaning to the child?
- When the behavior of a child harms others, do I attempt to apply Restorative Justice in a manner that may repair relationships?
- Do I approach the postdisciplinary conference with a caring attitude and a futuristic outlook focused upon new behaviors?
- Do I recognize when it is time to ask a team of concerned adults to complete an Abbreviated PTR for a child who has continuing maladaptive behavior patterns?
- Do I recognize when a child's behavior patterns have become so harmful to the child or others that team help or professional help is needed?
- Do I appreciate the fact that disciplinary interactions provide the opportunity for children to learn and grow into responsible adults?

Chapter Ten

Responding to Serious Misbehavior Patterns: Understanding the Purpose of Behavior

I n chapters 8 and 9 some basic principles of effective child discipline were introduced along with discipline strategies that are consistent with these principles. It is my hope that the knowledge learned in these two chapters can be helpful to parents and teachers as they address the common discipline problems that appear day to day in the lives of children. Sometimes, however, the extent of a child's misbehavior patterns is so extreme that the measures cited in these two chapters are not enough to bring about the changes a child needs to be successful in school or at home. Chapter 10 has been written to delve more deeply into the behavior of children who have not responded well to the normal behavior interventions tried by teachers and parents. The chapter begins with the story of a child whose behavior challenges called for a serious look into his past and a review of the many factors influencing his behavior:

> The most memorable event that I experienced in my twelve years of being an elementary principal at two schools occurred at Peavine Elementary School on the first day of school in 2005. On that day approximately $2,000 in cash was handed out to my students as they played tag and

slid down the slides on our playground. I was a little incredulous when a teacher brought a third grader to me who had a hundred-dollar bill that he said was given to him on the playground. It is not unusual for one child to bring money to school that he or she has found at home, so I was not stunned. Minutes later, however, I was shocked when three of our most responsible fifth graders brought me $200 in fifty-dollar bills they had been gifted on the playground. My first thought was that I had better do a tour of the playground to get my gift, but my inner self said I am the principal and I had better do something to get to the bottom of this.

You are probably anxious to know how this story ends! It turned out that a delayed older student was distributing funds he had found in his mother's freezer to all our students because he wanted to have friends at school. The unbridled honesty of most elementary school students was on display that day because I believe nearly all the money was returned to the boy's mother. After working with staff to retrieve as much money as we could, I settled into my office and pondered the discipline side of this issue. Do you discipline a child with developmental delays for distributing money at school to make friends?

My first thought was a question: *What was the purpose of this child's behavior?* As parents and teachers, if we can first understand the purpose of a child's behavior, we are better able to intervene with prevention, appropriate consequences and better teaching. After discussions with the boy, it was pretty clear that he wanted to have more friends because he needed to have a sense of "belonging" in our school. Because we learned that the boy's actions were motivated by his need for friends, we developed a plan to teach him how to make friends without spending money. An IEP team the next week added friendship skills into the boy's annual plan, and our counselor spent a considerable time with him over the next month. The next Saturday the boy spent ninety minutes cleaning our playground because that was the amount of time our custodian lost searching for money on the playground.

In the last decade the most prominent model for looking at student behavior in schools has been the PTR (prevent, teach, reinforce) system. An abbreviated form of this system was discussed in the previous chapter. The PTR model emphasizes the need of educators to gather useful data that can help establish the *function* of a student's behavior. In this context, I believe the function of student behavior and purpose of the behavior amount to the same thing. The real question is, "What does the student get from behaving in the manner he is behaving?" Once the school behavioral team develops a hypothesis about the function of a student's behavior, interventions are developed to teach and reinforce more appropriate behaviors that help these students satisfy their needs. When dealing with minor patterns of misbehavior, the abbreviated PTR can be a very useful template for organizing a successful intervention. *When dealing with more serious maladaptive behavior patterns such as routine aggression, a more elaborate PTR usually needs to occur with a considerable amount of time spent on establishing what the purpose of the child's behavior is.* The next section of this chapter is designed to assist adult teams attempting to discover the purpose of a child's pattern of misbehavior and to develop interventions that are designed to effectively respond to these purposeful behaviors.

There certainly is a disclaimer for those intending to use the PTR system to respond to serious misbehavior patterns. The PTR system may not work in all cases because of the varying reasons children have for misbehavior. For example, children with severe psychological or neurological issues may need additional therapy or medical interventions. The reality is that these children may be so disabled that they may need an entirely different approach to behavior change. Some of these obstacles to using the PTR system may become more obvious when the adult team struggles to determine the purpose of the child's misbehavior or the team decides that the child is not capable of changing his/her behavior without intensive community resources.

One of the first tasks facing a PTR team is to establish what the purpose of a child's behavior is. Psychologists, counselors, teachers, and parents have tried for centuries to better understand the purposeful function of child misbehavior. This is such an important endeavor because understanding the function of misbehavior leads to prevention and realistic interventions. There are no easy answers to this question, but there are some very interesting theories about the purposeful function of misbehavior that can be put to use by all of us. When I am reflecting about the function of a child's misbehavior or even *my own misbehavior*, I tend to ask myself the following questions:

1. Was the behavior influenced by some unmet need (like belonging) a person might have? *(Humanism)*
2. Was the behavior influenced by some deep-rooted emotions (typically, anger) that have overcome the person? *(Rogers' humanism)*
3. Was the behavior influenced by some faulty perceptions (e.g., the teacher hates me) or faulty thinking patterns? *(Cognitive learning theory)*
4. Does the person get rewarded (e.g., money buys friends) in some way for his/her behavior? *(Behaviorism)*

Each of these questions represents a different perspective for analyzing human behavior. Some of you are probably thinking that *all* these questions may be helpful to understand the purpose of the child's misbehavior. I agree, and I have spent most of my educational career asking all these questions (and a few more) whenever I have been asked to intervene with a child who has been misbehaving. All these questions represent a process for studying human behavior using different behavioral perspectives leading to effective interventions by caring adults. The unifying factor these approaches share is the need to *teach new social skills* once the causes of maladaptive behavior have been discovered, discussed, and addressed.

In order to answer these questions, the adult asking these questions must have some sort of data. Where does this data come from? Simply put, it comes from the actions and words of the child. This is when "active listening" becomes so important. What was the child thinking, wanting and feeling when he hit his brother? Were there any "pay-offs" to the child for hitting his brother? The answers to these questions can be provided to the adult by the child if a trusting relationship is established by the adult and he/she genuinely tries to understand the child's perspective on the events that have occurred. In addition, the adult who actively listens to a child conveys a level of respect to the child because the adult is communicating that he/she values the perspective of the child. This listening challenge may seem cumbersome, but it is vital if the adult is focused upon helping the child develop inner discipline and self-respect. The hope is the child will ask himself these same questions at a later date when he reflects upon his own actions.

I do hope the scenario I have presented helps to explain why discovering the purpose of child misbehavior is such an important endeavor. The remainder of this chapter will be focused upon helping the reader to gain a better understanding of the four perspectives about child behavior that I have mentioned, and how they can be used to develop meaningful interventions for children.

1. Human needs

Why does a baby cry when she is hungry? The answer is, of course, the baby is acting out because she has an unmet need for food. This is a key characteristic of humans that allows us to survive as a race. This same human characteristic, however, can lead us into trouble as we mature into adults. The most famous spokesperson for behavioral theories based upon human needs was Abraham Maslow, considered the father of humanistic psychology. In his book *Motivation and Personality* (1987), Maslow described five basic needs of all humans that must be satisfied if individuals are to become "self-actualized":

1. Physiological
2. Safety
3. Belongingness and love
4. Esteem
5. Self-actualization

Maslow presented these needs as a hierarchy in which the lower needs (beginning with physiological) have greater strength and importance. In a nutshell, Maslow contended that individuals who are stymied by a lower level need that is unfulfilled are unable to learn and progress as human beings. Their energies are diverted from improving themselves as human beings to deficiency need fulfillment at the lowest level. In very practical terms, Maslow would say that the child who goes to school hungry will not be a good learner that day.

Maslow's theories were very much in play when we discussed the behavior of our delayed student. On the first day of school his focus was upon "belonging" and not on the new types of math applications he was going to learn that year.

Parents and teachers who use Maslow's "lens" to analyze child misbehavior usually intervene by developing a plan to help the child address his deficiency need in an appropriate manner (Biehler and Snowman 1990). This is exactly what we did with our Peavine student. Make no mistake, the process of teaching new friendship skills was going to take a lot of time and commitment by the parent/teacher team working with this student.

I should spend a little more time discussing the "esteem" need that is near the top of Maslow's hierarchy. Countless psychologists such as Alfred Adler (Mosak 1973) have spent careers focusing upon self-esteem as the most important need we have as human beings. In earlier chapters I have discussed how important it is for children to have success in life because of their need for self-esteem. A learning disabled student who is failing in school may join a gang because he can be more successful committing crimes than writing essays.

Again, we must pay attention to the esteem needs of all children and help create an environment that allows the student to find success when effort is exerted.

Groups of educators attempting to understand the purpose of child misbehavior in the classroom have often preferred to concentrate on specific needs that children may have on a day-to-day basis in the classroom. These Adlerian needs may include the following:

- Attention
- Power/control
- Avoidance, escape

It is certainly true that many students will misbehave to gain attention or to avoid something. Over the years I have especially worried about low-achieving students who deliberately misbehave in order to be removed from a classroom environment that is painful to them. Some students, on the other hand, deliberately misbehave in the classroom or at home because they have learned to engage in power struggles with adults.

Rudolph Dreikurs (1991) suggested a way to determine the purpose of a child's behavior that has been of great use to me throughout my tenures as a counselor and principal. *Simply put, Dreikurs stated that you can usually determine the purpose of behavior by the way you feel during the interaction with a child.* If you are annoyed, the child may be acting out to get attention; if you are angry, you may be engaged in a power struggle with the child and if you feel hurt, the child may be seeking revenge. I have found these "gut checks" to be extremely useful in my quest to understand the behavior of different children.

2. Deep-rooted emotions

Have you ever acted unreasonably because you were overwhelmed by an emotion? I know I have, and I suspect most of you have too. In a sense, our behavior becomes an outlet for our emotions. For example, a parent who has had an upsetting day at work may be quicker to spank a child for being late to the dinner table. Sadly, the function of this parent's behavior can be interpreted to be an outlet for overwhelming emotions instead of a meaningful response to tardiness. In these types of cases the child often learns more from the parent example of poor emotional self-control than he or she learns from the spanking punishment.

A remarkable characteristic of most human beings is that they can often gain "control" of an emotion simply by recognizing and *expressing* the emotion. If one could go back in time, the spanking parent may have responded differently to his child's misbehavior if his spouse had talked about his day with him and empathized with his frustration at work. Having someone to help us identify our emotions and attempt to understand them can be a powerful anecdote to losing self-control.

Carl Rogers reformed the entire counseling field when he introduced the concept that counselors can best help individuals solve their own problems by forming a trusting relationship with these individuals and demonstrating empathy in every way possible. One of the key features of Rogers's theory was that helping a distressed individual to understand and express his emotions is a precursor to effective problem-solving.

Parents and teachers attempting to understand the function of a child's behavior should never ignore the power of emotions. One does not have to be a Carl Rogers–trained counselor to sit down with a child, listen to her and use empathic responses to help the child gain control of her emotions, and ultimately, her behavior. This is not an easy process, *but it is crucial that children learn how to recognize and control their emotions if they are ever to develop inner discipline.*

Recognizing and dealing with deep-seated emotions is much more challenging than dealing with short-term emotional outbursts. In many cases the teachers and parents who understand that a child is consumed by emotions such as anger, guilt or resentment may need guidance counseling or therapy. The act of listening to these children is a powerful intervention, but sometimes these children need more services than we can provide them alone.

Unfortunately, some children struggle expressing their emotions because of language delays. I would like to present an example of a child who faced this problem and what was done to help him:

> Tony was a big first grader at Lemmon Valley School in Reno who was often in trouble for hitting other students and having emotional outbursts in class. When Tony was sent to the office, it was very difficult to understand him because of his severe expressive language delays. His parents were very cooperative with school staff and wanted help for their son. It was interesting, and somewhat diagnostic, that Tony's fourth-grade brother was calm and never in trouble. A child study team developed a hypothesis that Tony's misbehavior was primarily caused by his inability to express himself literally and emotionally and the resulting tensions this caused. The team worked very hard with our speech/language therapists and his parents to help Tony develop better expressive language skills and a "feelings" vocabulary. By the time Tony was a third grader, his behavior had normalized at school because he was now able to express his emotions instead of lashing out when he was frustrated.

In summary, it is very important for teachers and parents trying to understand the purpose of a child's behavior to make every effort to help the child understand the emotions that may have played a big part of the misbehavior that has occurred. The emotional context of misbehavior is usually not the only factor to consider, but it is an important factor that can never be ignored.

3. Perceptions and beliefs

> When I was fourteen, it seemed to me that my
> parents did not know anything. By the time I was
> twenty-one, I was impressed by how much they
> had learned.
>
> —Mark Twain

Mark Twain aptly reminds us that childhood perceptions are influenced by many factors, and they do change over time. Sometimes the act of understanding a child's perception and basic thoughts may give listening adults clues to understanding the purpose of a child's behavior. The basic premise behind this approach is that there is usually a conscious thought between an event and our emotional response (Beck 1976). For example, I remember recently talking to a little second grader at Mariposa Academy who had shown sudden signs of withdrawal in his classroom. The teacher suspected his parent's upcoming divorce was a significant factor influencing this change in behavior:

> It took about twenty minutes of rapport building with Jose before I felt I could begin to ask him penetrating questions. He freely talked with me and quickly brought our conversation to his parents' impending divorce. It turned out he was blaming himself for the divorce because he continuously heard his parents argue about child care, transporting to school and extracurricular activities. When we talked about school, Jose said he was so concerned about his own care and worried about his parents' breakup that sometimes he "drifted off" in class. After a conversation with Jose's parents, it became clear that the school withdrawal could best be addressed by some short-term family counseling and a concerted effort by the parents to assure Jose that he was

not to blame for his parent's divorce and his parents would still take care of him after the divorce.

Jose had a limited "snapshot" of his parent's relationship, and he had interpreted it based upon his narrow experiences as an eight-year-old boy. His thoughts about the impending divorce were leading to emotions of sorrow, guilt and worry. It would now be up to the important adults in Jose's life to listen to him and to broaden his perspective on the divorce. Once Jose can relieve himself from his guilt and get reassurance that his parents will provide for his welfare in a new manner, there is a good chance his classroom activity will pick up again. This is a good example of how our thinking patterns can affect our emotions and our behavior. This is true for Jose, but it is also true for all of us, no matter what our age is.

At this point I would list some examples of unhelpful perceptions that I have observed and discussed with young children in the past few years:

- It is my fault my parents are divorcing. I don't care anymore.
- I can't read very well, so I must be dumb and there is no need to try.
- No matter how hard I try, I fail. It's not worth trying.
- I must be a bad person because nobody likes me.
- My teacher hates me because she is always mad at me.
- It is awful to fail a test. I am afraid I will be retained.
- Tommy called me fat. I will be embarrassed the rest of my life.
- If the students laugh at me in class, it means they like me.
- If I can't please my parents, why try? I'll just try to please my friends.
- I will never love another girl as much as I loved Mary.
- If I were to die, nobody would care.

Note: The comments from the last student partly resulted in a suicide intervention protocol being implemented to help the child. The outcomes were good in this case.

As heartbreaking as some of these beliefs are, they can be very real to the child holding on to these beliefs and often lead to hurtful emotions and misbehavior. Equally important, understanding these beliefs can be the key factor in understanding the purpose of a child's behavior and the development of future interventions.

Helping children review and change their beliefs

> We must remember that although a child is an excellent observer, he is a very poor interpreter and needs someone to put his observations in proper perspective
>
> —Rudolph Dreikurs

Tamar Chansky (2009) in his book *Freeing Your Child from Negative Thinking* provides a very useful quotation that can help the reader understand the foundation of cognitive learning theory for children:

> While we can't control the events that happen to us, we can control the story we tell ourselves about those events, and therefore we hold the key to the effect they have on us.

If one accepts Chansky's premise, the job of supportive adults is to assist children to tell themselves a "story" about events that is realistic and helpful. For example, the child who is telling himself that he is a bad person because nobody likes him may need assistance to understand that he is not a "bad" person; instead, he just needs help to learn and practice good friend-making behaviors. Similarly, the learning disabled (LD) student who thinks he is dumb because he cannot read may benefit from hearing stories of successful LD individuals such as Albert Einstein and Winston Churchill who succeeded because they had many strengths outside of reading that they put to use in magnificent ways.

The path to helping children understand and challenge their beliefs is not an easy one. In my experiences younger children are much more amenable to this process than older students because their beliefs are still formative and not as entrenched as most teenagers present. The key steps to assisting a child examine his or beliefs include the following:

1. Build a trusting relationship with the child with a focus upon active listening.
2. Attempt to understand any faulty beliefs that may be interfering with the child's success.
3. Test your hypothesis about faulty beliefs by asking the child if he agrees with you. Discuss the reasons why the faulty belief is not reasonable.
4. Help the child to generate a new belief that is more realistic and helpful.
5. Discuss the new feelings and behaviors that the realistic belief may help influence.

In Jose's case, he actually began crying when I asked him if he was afraid that his parents would not get him to school or have a babysitter for him at night. He truly believed that he would not be taken care of after the divorce. Once we replaced his belief that his parents would not provide for his general welfare with a belief that he would be well taken care of but in *a different* manner, he became more relaxed and ready to participate in school.

The happiness equation

In his book *Authentic Happiness* (2017), Martin Seligman suggests that there is a strong connection between our beliefs/thoughts and our happiness. He presents a formula for measuring happiness that intuitively makes sense to me although I cannot say it is thoroughly research-based. The formula is

$Happiness = Set + Circumstances + Voluntary$
$Control$, or $H = S + C + V$

Seligman defines *set* to be our genetic tendencies or inborn factors such as temperament and *circumstances* to be life events such as poor health, income, report cards, etc. *Voluntary control* is the pivotal factor because it involves our thinking processes and the "story" we tell ourselves. If one accepts Seligman's theory about happiness, it becomes very evident that how we think about an event or a circumstance is a crucial factor in determining the happiness we have in life. For example, my willingness to view my cancer as a life-changing circumstance (*C*) that has filled my life with gratitude and appreciation (*V*) has served to increase my happiness (*H*) when compared to an attitude of resentment about an unfair circumstance that derailed my life. Taking this analysis a bit further, Sonja Lyubomirsky (2013) and her colleagues from the University of California have used their own research to quantify Seligman's equation to look like this:

$$H = .50S + .10C + .40V$$

An entire book can be written about this equation, but the important idea is that how we process or think about an event or circumstance is more important than the circumstance itself. The assertion that how we view (*V*) a circumstance influences about 40 percent of our resulting happiness makes sense to me based upon my experiences as an educator and parent. The challenge is, of course, to help children develop a healthy *V* factor.

The process of helping children develop a healthy *V* factor goes way beyond the particular event or circumstance at hand. In fact, one of the key variables predicting childhood inner discipline must be the ability to respond to an unfortunate event with realistic and helpful thinking. Will the young boy who just lost a soccer game push one of his opponents as he leaves the field or will he see the loss as a temporary setback and start to think about what the team can do better next week? Having a healthy *V* will be a determining factor in this decision. In fact, one can see that helping children to develop a healthy *V* factor is an important element leading to childhood resiliency in the face of disappointing events in life.

I believe there are two crucial factors that can help children to improve their *V* factor:

1. Living with adults who *model* effective *V* behavior. In fact, the idea of teachers and parents sharing their thinking out loud in front of children does not seem out of line to me. Can you imagine a parent who says at the dinner table, "Right now I am angry at your teacher, so after dinner I am going to take a walk in order to reorganize myself and try to think of some ideas that can help the teacher do her job and you (the student) do your job."

2. The presence of adults who practice active listening with a child in a manner that encourages the child to challenge his or her thinking. The initial goal of this process is, of course to help the child develop realistic and helpful perspectives on the issues at hand. *The ultimate goal is helping the child to develop the resources to challenge his or her own thinking when crises occur.*

I am reminded that changing perceptions and beliefs is not an easy process—it takes patience. Some writers suggest that changing a person's perception about events in his/ her life may take *one month for every year a perception has been in place* (Fay and Fay 1995).

In summary, there is no doubt that the adults attempting to help a child change his or her behavior will have a better chance of success if they understand the "thinking" behind the child's behavior. In this section of the chapter several examples have been provided of childhood faulty thinking that often lead to hurtful emotions and misbehavior. It is the job of parents and teachers to help children challenge this faulty thinking and to help children develop thinking patterns that are realistic and helpful. *Eventually, it is the hope that children will learn to challenge their own thinking and develop "stories" about events that help them to become resilient in times of crises.*

4. *Behavior learning theory*

Were you surprised when Aaron, the boy with an angry alcoholic father, left his suspension meeting with a smug look on his face? After all, he was being suspended from school for two days! I have seen this look before on students being suspended, and I believe I know why the expected tears and outrage stemming from school suspensions seldom appear nowadays. In a nutshell, suspension often means two days of enjoyable video games and TV watching instead of school work—what a deal! The consequence for Aaron's behavior had no effect on him because suspension was almost a reward. This scenario leads to one of the major principles of B. F. Skinner's learning theory; namely, *the consequence of a behavior often determines if the behavior will occur again.* That is to say, if the behavior is rewarded, it is likely to continue or increase and if the behavior has a negative consequence, it is likely to decrease. In cases like this the *purpose* of the behavior is to earn the reward the behavior produces. I would like to provide some common examples of this principle in homes and schools:

1. The child who is jealous of his mother's attention misbehaves in order to get his mother's negative attention (reward). A similar pattern may occur in the classroom with the child's teacher.
2. The student who struggles with math teases his friend during math instruction so that he will be rewarded by removal from class during math.
3. The student who does not do well in school is sick a lot so he does not have to go to school.
4. The student who has no friends at recess does not do her homework so the teacher will reward her by having her miss recess doing homework.
5. The teenager who makes a big scene about doing the dishes because he knows his parents will eventually give up on the dishes requirement.

Certainly, all of us can relate to these examples of cases in which a child's misbehavior is a function of the consequences that occur following the behavior. Many times the child is very conscious of the relationship between the behavior and its consequences, but other times the connection is subconscious. In either case, it is very important for adults attempting to help children change patterns of misbehavior to examine the consequences of the misbehavior to see if, in fact, these consequences can be changed in a way that does not reward the misbehavior.

When I was a first year principal at Lemmon Valley Elementary School, I remember in September having about thirty discipline referrals sent to my office a day. This was too many referrals for a school of 750 students! I soon realized that some kids liked sitting in the office instead of the classroom and the kids who were suspended for serious infractions didn't seem to mind being suspended to their home. In October two new rules were instituted by me with staff approval:

1. If a student committed a serious infraction, he or she would attend a three-hour Saturday school in my office involving reading, writing and school cleanup.
2. If a student was asked to leave class because of disruptive behavior, he or she would spend an hour after school in detention doing missed schoolwork.

These discipline changes resulted in a 50 percent decrease in discipline referrals the first month. Of course, successful school discipline is a multifaceted process that involves much more than consequences, but I have to tell you these two rule changes made a significant impact on our school discipline immediately because misbehavior was no longer being rewarded.

There is another side to this story. When you go to Las Vegas or Reno, which casino do you tend to visit first? Of course, you visit the casino you previously won in. This example illustrates a second principle of learning theory: namely, *a behavior that is rewarded continues or increases its frequency.* The reward of winning in a casino increases the likelihood you will revisit the casino. This behavioral principle is very real for all humans, but especially for children. If you have a system that is rewarding for new behaviors, they are more likely to occur.

This principle was certainly in play for Jacob, a student in Marvin Moss Elementary School in Sparks, Nevada, who bullied others on the playground because he had no idea how to manage conflicts. After the intervention team taught him new skills, they made every effort possible to reward him when he demonstrated the new skills. When he was observed by a Duty teacher settling a tether ball dispute by negotiating a win-win solution, his counselor was notified and held a praiseful review session with him. I learned later that Jacob's teacher took the time to call home about the successful conflict resolution.

Thus, parents and teachers trying to determine the purpose of a student's behavior should always be prepared to analyze the consequences that follow the behavior. Sometimes the easiest interventions to help children improve their behavior involve manipulation of behavior consequences.

Summary

The crux of this chapter is certainly the idea that behavior is purposeful, and understanding the purpose of behavior can help adults to intervene in ways that are helpful to misbehaving children. This process involves some keen listening as a child tells his/her story, and a review of the circumstances surrounding the child's behaviors.

Understanding the function of a child's behavior is not an easy task. It involves using questioning strategies that explore a child's needs, thinking, emotions, skills, and the consequences that follow a child's behavior. Parents and teachers who are willing to undertake the time it takes to really understand the function of a child's behavior will always have more long-term success helping the child improve his or her behavior compared to adults who select short-term punishments alone.

Pause and reflect

Sometimes I stand in awe of the power of children to change their ways and adapt to shifting circumstances. This is a human characteristic that involves evolving life perspectives, emotional growth, social learning and self-understanding. It is a process that does not happen by itself and we, as parents and teachers, have been blessed with the opportunity to guide and support children as they go through their individual learning process. Some questions we may wish to ask of ourselves include:

Parents and teachers

- Do I respond to serious misbehavior in a punishing manner, or do I respond to this misbehavior in a *multifaceted manner* that attempts to penetrate the forces that drove the behavior in the first place?
- Do I recognize that all behavior is *purposeful?* Am I willing to go beyond the first layer of behavior to try to understand underlying factors that influence the behavior?
- Do I believe that all children can learn to behave appropriately with the right supports, teaching, and encouragement
- Do I *listen to* the children I live with and work with? Have I made an effort to understand the thoughts, needs, feelings and consequences that influence their behavior?
- Do I take the time to understand and address the emotions behind a child's misbehavior before moving to a problem-solving mode?
- Do I model appropriate self-control and flexible perceptions for my children? Do I ever share my inner thoughts or emotions with my children in a constructive manner?
- Am I rewarding inappropriate behavior in any manner? Am I rewarding behavior change?
- Do I responded to misbehavior in a thoughtful manner that will help the child to develop his or her own *inner discipline?*

- Do I take the time to stand back and appreciate the effort many children make to improve themselves and become responsible citizens?

Chapter Eleven

Intensive-Care Children

May your weeds grow up to be wildflowers.
—Georgia O'Keeffe

Every spring I take a walk that has me cross the railroad tracks and climb an embankment. At the top of the embankment is an ugly weed that most people would remove if it popped up in their back-yard. This weed receives no human attention, very little water and it looks prickly. The first time I saw this weed, I admired its resiliency because it, alone, had survived the winter snow and summer heat, whereas no other plants had made it in the hard, unforgiving soil it lived in. I now know something about this weed that others will probably never know—it has the most beautiful bloom in June. Is it a beautiful weed or a hidden wildflower? The answer to this question is unimportant. What is important is that this plant has an indom-itable strength and a hidden beauty that sometimes we cannot see. I eagerly look to see if this plant has survived the winter on my first walk each spring, and it never disappoints me.

The metaphor of the wildflower can be used to explain my beliefs about children who are continually in trouble or need lots of extra care to be successful in their school and home ventures. Every teacher has a few of these children in their classroom and most par-ents who have multiple children have one child who struggles more than others with family dynamics. These children are the children who never miss school and demand much attention from parents and teachers, alike. It is my belief that the best way to help these children to succeed in life is to make an extra effort to discover the "bloom" that each of these children possesses. Said in a better way, we must strive to find the "buried treasure" that lies within each of these children (Levine 2002).

What distinguishes these children from other children is that they are *"intensive care"* (IC) *children* who, just like in the hospital, need more services and extra care until their behavior becomes adaptive, successful and not harmful to others. I like the term IC children because it does not imply permanent disabilities or limits on success; instead, the term suggests that at this time in their lives, these children need extra care to be successful in their day to day struggles. Many of these IC children have behavior problems associated with their challenging circumstances, but some do not. *The ultimate goal for IC children is to give them extensive care now, so that later in life they can give themselves the care that they need to be successful in life.*

Chapter 11 is really a chapter about the process of helping the majority of IC children who persist with maladaptive behaviors despite the best efforts of concerned parents and teachers who daily interact with them. The overriding message of the chapter, however, is the reality that children with special needs in their life can survive to be successful contributors to our society if the important adults in their life give them the intensive care they need when they need it most.

Like the harsh soil my renegade weed lives in, these IC children may have experienced ineffective parenting, abuse, divorce, trauma, learning disabilities, medical issues, and many other factors that might have contributed to their setback as thriving children. Some of these children are angry and blaming others, while others are silently blaming themselves. What often binds these children together is a series of behaviors that are not helping each one of them to become responsible adults with inner discipline. Hence, one can say that the "bloom" of these children has remained hidden and the prickly thorns are usually very visible.

It is beyond the scope of this book to present a treatise about the varied strategies available to help children exhibiting maladaptive behavior. In some cases, the best source of help available for parents struggling with children exhibiting maladaptive behaviors is to seek the help of counselors and family therapists who work with children displaying behavior problems on a daily basis. This being said, there will be an emphasis in this chapter on some of the common themes that parents working with therapists and teachers working with guidance counselors will probably be introduced to during their consulting sessions. In this chapter six themes will be discussed:

1. Forgiveness, hope, and patience
2. Taming the spirited child
3. The emotional bank account
4. Setting limits and enforcing them
5. Special educators got it right!
6. Reality checks

Before delving into these themes in more depth, it is important to point out that all the principles of parenting foundations and effective discipline mentioned in previous chapters certainly apply to these IC children exhibiting maladaptive behaviors. At this point in their life, however, the IC children need more than just good discipline—they need extra care.

I. Forgiveness, faith, and patience

> Every saint has a past and every sinner has a future.
> —Oscar Wilde

There is no question that IC children are difficult to deal with. They often take a disproportionate amount of teacher time and they worry parents. Sometimes they call us names and complain that we are mean. Teachers often bemoan the fact that when their most IC child is absent, life is so smooth in class.

The first task of teachers and parents who want to help IC children is to forgive them for their "thorns." Given some of the hateful things teenagers can say to their parents or teachers, this can be a hard thing to do. Honestly, I often try to remember Oscar Wilde's quote when I am in these situations. I try to recall my sins as a teenager in the past and I am glad others have forgiven me. More important, I try to reach back and find the optimism in my soul that will allow me to have faith that each IC child can have a bright future with proper guidance from the important adults in his or her life. The scenario presented below illustrates the importance of key adults believing in the ability of children to make positive changes in their life:

> The first-grade teachers are meeting with the second-grade teachers to assign students into their second grade classroom for next year. The subject of Johnny, a challenging IC student, causes each teacher to stop and pause. Mrs. Jones strongly announces she does not want Johnny in her class because of his disruptive behavior. After a nerve-raking twenty seconds, Mrs. Smith says she would like to have Johnny in her class because she thinks she can help him and likes his spirit. The grade-level decision is made to put Johnny in Mrs. Smith's class, but to also assign her two less students than the other teachers.

These types of discussions happen in May in schools throughout the country. If you were Johnny's mother, which class would you want him in? Of course, you would want him in Mrs. Smith's classroom. The research on behavior-disordered children supports the placement of Johnny in Mrs. Smith's classroom because this research suggests that the "attitude" of teachers trying to educate behavior-disordered children is the key predictor of behavioral success in classrooms. If teachers and parents are going to have success with IC students, they must believe in the capacity of these children to change their ways and they must have faith that these IC children can "bloom" in the future. We can never "give up" on these children.

Mrs. Smith believes she can help Johnny change his ways. This belief in Johnny will go a long ways, but it is not sufficient to see the change she wants to see. She will need help and guidance from school staff and, hopefully, parental support. Additionally, Mrs. Smith will need to have patience. As has been mentioned in previous chapters, perceptions need time to change and new behaviors must be practiced many times before they become natural for a child. I am reminded of the wisdom we can all learn from the old jewelry diamond cutters in previous centuries:

> The diamond cutters spent a great deal of time hammering each diamond precisely before the diamond would fracture in the right manner. Sometimes the diamond would need to be hit one hundred times before it fractured correctly. When the diamond cutter celebrated his success, he knew that each one of the one hundred hits counted for something even though success came way later.

Mrs. Smith and Johnny's mother will need to understand that Johnny will need lots of interventions at home and in school before he is ready to become the beautiful cut "diamond" he can become. The intersection of faith, teaching/parenting skills, caring, and patience will be the intensive care that Johnny will need to find a path of success in life.

2. Taming the spirited child

> It is much easier to find ways to get a spirited child to manage his enormous energy effectively than it is to breathe life into a passive child.
>
> —Popkin 2007

It's early September in a first grade classroom at Lemmon Valley School. The six-year-old first graders are learning to adjust to the tall, gruff male teacher with a loud voice (caused by his hearing loss). Later the kids will come to love this teacher, but right now there is some cautious fear. Similarly, the teacher is adjusting to the personalities and academic levels of the twenty-five squirming first graders going to school for a full day for the first time in their lives. When the teacher assigns each student to read a pre-primer passage to his seat partner, Billy runs out of the room and takes off. It turns out that Billy never learned a letter in kindergarten and he could never begin to read a passage at this point in his life. Billy was also very afraid of his new teacher! Staff looked for Billy for about thirty minutes and called his father. When the police were about to be called, Billy was found under a car with wires in his hands. He was, in fact, rewiring the car and, guess what, it was his new teacher's car!

The story of Billy is a story I have repeated many times, and each time I tell the story I have a new "take" on the events that took place that fall morning. One factor about this story has remained constant for me, however, and that is the fact that I have always admired Billy's "spirit." It took a lot of gumption for Billy to race out of class, find the teacher's car and begin his project. It would be our job in the coming months to harness that spirit and point-it in a positive direction.

The heading of this section is directly taken from a wonderful book by Dr. Michael Popkin (2007) titled *Taming the Spirited Child: Strategies for Parenting Challenging Children without Breaking Their Spirits*. The title of this book says it all. It is our job as parents and teachers to appreciate the spirit of each child and to help these children navigate the challenges of society so that their spirit can be on full display and inspiring to all of us. Forgive me for using a sports analogy, but it does seem fitting in this case. Willie Mays probably had more raw talent and a "unique" spirit than any other rookie baseball player in his day, but he went zero for twenty-four in his first bats. It took the encouragement of a manager who ignored the batting average because he recognized Willie's talent to help him become the greatest player of all time. With guidance, Willie had to learn to pace himself, take pitches, deal with disappointment and believe in himself before his real talents began to win games for the Giants. Not all of our IC children will become the Willie Mays of our generation, but each of these children has a spirit and talent waiting to be discovered and set free by an encouraging adult. In a sense, these children need to be guided in a manner that allows them *to find their voice and to be proud of themselves.*

In his book, Dr. Popkin emphasizes appreciating and utilizing your child's strengths, encouragement, understanding the purpose of misbehavior and responding to misbehavior in a calm, purposeful manner. Many of these suggestions were put in play when we discussed Billy's situation in a child-study team:

- We easily decided Billy's behavior was guided by a need to escape from his embarrassment about being a nonreader. We also learned that Billy frequently did not understand situations and running was a normal behavior for him.
- Billy's teacher readily accepted that he needed to learn more about Billy and to not put Billy and other nonreaders in awkward situations.
- Billy was assessed and determined to be in need of special education academic and language services. These services began right away.
- Billy's teacher admired his spirit and tried to be very encouraging to him. We did not have an auto-mechanics class for first graders, but all of Billy's teachers tried to find ways he could express himself with his hands. We had strong suspicions that Billy's *voice* in life would somehow involve his hands.
- Our counselor and speech language therapist worked to help Billy find better ways to communicate his feelings and deal with frustration appropriately.
- Billy apologized to his teacher and stayed after school for thirty minutes to help clean the teacher's room. The two talked a lot during this time and improved their relationship.

- The teacher no longer parked his car near his classroom.

There were a lot of interventions implemented to help Billy. None of these interventions, however, would have been effective if the teacher and staff had not come to *appreciate* Billy's spirit and hidden talents as an important first grader in our school.

3. The emotional bank account

The concept of the emotional bank account (EBA) was first introduced by Stephen Covey in his famous book *The 7 Habits of Highly Effective People* (1989). In his book, Stephen Covey uses the metaphor of a bank savings account to explain how important it is for leaders to build a level of trust with their team members. When a leader does something that inspires trust from others, he/she is making a savings deposit of trust into an account. The corollary to this deposit is, of course, that withdrawals are made from the account when leaders do something that is not trust inspiring. The goal is to make enough deposits into the account that a reserve is built and the leader's account can stay positive even when withdrawal crises occur.

I truly believe that the EBA concept can apply to parenting and teaching in a manner that goes well beyond trust. It can be used as a strategy to simply strengthen the relationship between a child and his parents or teacher. When a parent takes his child to the movies, a relationship deposit is being made in the EBA, or when a teacher goes to a basketball game to root for one of his/her students, an EBA relationship deposit is being made. The great value of these EBA deposits is the fact that they provide a reserve when problems occur. The teenager who is very angry with his parents for not being allowed to go to his friend's party may have an easier time accepting the decision when there is a positive EBA reserve between his parents and himself.

Why is the emotional bank account such an important focus in our discussions of IC children? The sad reality is that most parents and teachers of IC children have a *negative balance in their EBA* because they have had to discipline these children so much. I can't tell you how many times I have heard the parents of IC children complain that they do not enjoy parenting anymore because they are always restricting or "grounding" their children. We usually talk about these issues in great length, but one question I often ask is, "When was the last time you took your kid shopping, to a game or to a concert?" The point I try to make when I ask these questions is the fact that having a savings reserve of positive experiences in your EBA is of huge importance when dealing with children and their sensitive issues.

Parents and teachers who genuinely want to make deposits in their EBA with children can do many things to make these deposits:

> When my son and I were having some relationship difficulties during his teenage years, we would go to the Cal-Neva on Sundays to have the $1.99 steak/eggs breakfast and put down a four-team football parlay. My sister did something I would be hard-pressed to do: she went to Metallica concerts with her sixteen-year-old-son.

Stephen Covey (1989) talks about other forms of deposits that are not as obvious but just as important: "understanding the individual, attending to little things, keeping commitments, clarifying expectations, showing personal integrity and apologizing when you make a withdrawal." All in all, making deposits into the EBA of IC children is a good thing to do, it is the right thing to do and it can be fun! It is marvelous to think that having fun with your child or student is good parenting or good teaching.

When I was a principal I heard a phrase at a workshop that I really took to heart. The speaker said that one can predict that your delinquent sixth graders may be in jail by nineteen and your failing sixth-grade students will be high school dropouts by nineteen. Recognizing that these broad predictions to have some validity, I considered my failing and delinquent sixth graders to be IC children. As a group of educators and parents, we needed to help turn these children in another direction soon in order to defeat this frightening prediction. Our team interventions to help these children were varied, but one thing I did was to take some of these IC children to UNR basketball games and other events. My wife and I enjoyed doing this with the kids, but I was also contributing to my EBA with each of these students. I knew someday I would have to make EBA withdrawals with some of these students, and I wanted a reserve to build upon.

4. Setting limits and enforcing them

> Warmth never supersedes discipline, nor discipline warmth.
>
> —William Glasser

Have you ever walked into a classroom or home where it was clear that no limits on behavior had been set? It can be a really awkward experience that is not fun. I want to let you in on a secret—classrooms without limits are uncomfortable for adults to observe, but they are also uncomfortable for the children who participate in the chaos. I learned this important concept when I worked in a class for high school students with disabilities at Bishop Manogue Catholic High School. The students who came to our room would complain quite a bit about the few classrooms they attended that did not have effective behavior limits. Although these students thought some of the disruptive behavior in these classrooms was funny, these same students wanted more stability from their teachers. Luckily, the administration did listen to the students about these rare situations.

I think it is fair to say that all children want limits on behavior. These limits provide security for children and they help guide the behavior of the children. It is like having a backyard with a fence around it. The fence protects the children from intruders; it does not allow them to get lost, but it does not restrict how they play within the yard.

Parents and teachers are expected to set the limits for their classrooms and homes. The limit-setting process can go many ways depending on the age of the children but it should usually include input from the children and have a focus upon order and the Right Triangle mentioned in previous chapters. Of course, limits need to be reasonable, in-tune with the school or family mission and flexible enough to change as children mature. Discussions about rules and limits should be encouraged, especially with older children. The process of setting limits must be followed by clarification of these limits and a "teaching" process that culminates with the children knowing exactly what is expected of them.

Dr. James Dobson (1992) makes a powerful statement about rule discussions and managing teenagers when he says, "Give them maximum reason to comply with your wishes." Clearly, Dr. Dobson believed that parents should take the time to explain the reasons behind the rules in order to solicit teenager "buy-in" to the rules. Lastly, the limits set by parents and teachers must be *enforced consistently*.

What is the "magic formula" for raising and educating IC children who have behavior problems? It is the same formula that all children benefit from: develop reasonable rules and enforce them in a calm and consistent manner. *The sad reality of this situation is that many IC children have been deprived of this magic formula either because of poor limit setting or inconsistent enforcement.* These same IC children can thrive in an environment that has fair rules that are administered consistently with ample time for good two-way discussions about behavior. Reasonable rules must be *enforced* in a manner that still allows the adult's level of caring to shine through. Often times, it is the discussion that occurs much later after the consequences have been applied that helps the child to understand the level of care and concern the parent or teacher has for the child.

5. Special educators got it right!

I believe that is fair to say that many IC children have behavioral problems in school or at home. Certainly this is not the case with all IC children, but it is true for many IC children because they may have unfulfilled needs that are driving their behavior in negative ways. A certain percentage of these students are made eligible for special education services because of "emotional disturbance," learning disabilities or other specified disabilities.

During my days as a special education director I often heard comments about the "protected" status of children with disabilities. This was true because special education law *limits* suspension days if a student's behavior is related to his handicap and the law *requires* school/parent teams to develop a plan to address the student's misbehavior "Why is it that our hands are tied when we try to discipline children with disabilities?" This comment and other similar comments were often offhandedly spoken in my office. It has always been my contention that the educators, legislators, parents and judges weighing in on present day special education laws got it *right* and the rest of us have often gotten it *wrong. Special education laws require that a "teaching model" be used to discipline children with disabilities. What a novel concept!*

Special education laws governing the discipline of children have steadfastly expected that educators who discipline children with maladaptive behavior patterns take the time to address a student's behavior in his or her Individual Education Plan (Gorn 1997). In other words, educators and parents are expected to work together to develop an educational plan that proactively addresses the child's misbehavior and teaches adaptive behaviors. What a simple but wonderful idea! If a child is commonly misbehaving, teachers and principals should assess this misbehavior from an educational perspective. This process has been described in earlier chapters and identified as the PTR model. An example of this PTR process for a student with disabilities occurred in a rural high school I was serving as a school psychologist:

> I was contacted by the high school special education teacher who was extremely upset that one of his students had been suspended for a week by the school vice principal because he told his shop teacher to "get f——d." It turned out that the student was moderately mentally retarded because of a car accident that had left his face severely emaciated and injured his brain. It was

also presented at the meeting that two other students had dared him to take the actions he did. We immediately had an IEP meeting with the teacher(s), vice principal and a foster parent. At the meeting it was determined that the student's behavior was related to his disability and the suspension was unreasonable.

The IEP team gathered more information and determined that the boy would need counseling regarding peer influence on an ongoing basis. In fact, ninety minutes of counseling per month were added to the IEP and the boy's special education teacher agreed to spend more time working on peer decision-making in his social skills curriculum. The boy did have quite a discussion with his counselor and he did apologize to his teacher in a very tearful manner after staying home for one day. The IEP team was required by law to develop a proactive plan to help this student improve his behavior; nevertheless, we created a plan to help this student because we believed *it was the right thing to do.*

The notion that repeated childhood misbehavior can best be addressed by using a PTR model should not be limited to children with disabilities. In this case, the legal requirements that protect children with disabilities and require an IEP team to address the child's behavior are requirements that should be applied to *all* children who have serious patterns of misbehavior in school. I guarantee you if this occurred, we would see improved behavior in our schools and fewer IC children needing services.

6. Reality checks

> The patient must decide the irresponsibility of
> behavior, not the therapist.
>
> —William Glasser

In recent years two authors have had a profound effect upon my thinking about IC children. These authors, Susan Scott (2002) and William Glasser (1965), came from different times in our history, and their books speak to different audiences, but their central message is essentially the same: *we must be able to confront the realities of our situation and help others confront their own realities.* Both authors tend to agree that people struggling with personal issues tend to hide from the realities of their situation because of unmet needs or an unwillingness to engage in "fierce conversations" (Scott 2002). Polite conversations that produce little change and superficial relationships are frequently the outcome when individuals are unwilling to confront the realities they are facing. Of course, both authors strongly suggest that the best way to help individuals face their problems is to have authentic conversations that are reality based. In this book those conversations will be called "reality checks." In this section of the book I will discuss two types of reality checks: (1) adults questioning whether or not their system of discipline is working and (2) adults helping children to judge the realities of their own behavior.

A. Adult reality checks

> All life is an experiment. The more experiments
> you make the better.
>
> —Ralph Waldo Emerson

Is your system for disciplining this child working? I cannot tell you how many times I have asked this question of exhausted parents or beleaguered teachers. The response I get after a long pause is usually, "Not really." It turns out that many adults are very adept at describing what they do to respond to child misbehavior, but these same adults are not very good at questioning the effectiveness of their approach. The teacher who continually sends students from her class to the office without seeing behavior change is just as guilty as the parent who continues to spank his/her child without changes in behavior. Both parties have avoided asking themselves the big question: Is my approach working? This form of reality check is something parents and teachers need to do frequently if they are determined to provide children the guidance they need to develop inner discipline.

When dealing with IC children, the answer to the reality check question may sometimes be "not really." If this is the case, it is time to reorganize and review your approach to see what is working and what is not working. Sometimes it is helpful to brainstorm with a friend or professional. It might even be helpful to have this conversation with the child in a calm and thoughtful manner. The important point here is that you recognize changes must be made, and you are willing to begin a process to discover better approaches to parenting or teaching for the child of concern. Listed below are some considerations you may wish to think about:

1. How is your relationship with the child? Are you taking the time to show the child how much you care for him/her? Is there an EBA positive balance?
2. Are your rules reasonable, flexible, fair, and enforced justly?
3. Do you model and teach your expectations?
4. Do you take the time to have frequent discussions with the child about his/her behavior in good times and in bad times?
5. Are your consequences reasonable, consistently enforced and meaningful? Are the consequences helping to change behavior?
6. Would an Abbreviated PTR team process be helpful as a way to develop new interventions? Do you readily understand the purpose of the child's misbehavior?
7. Does the child need more help than you can provide him?

There are no easy answers to childhood discipline in schools and in homes. Perhaps it is best to remember Ralph Waldo Emerson's quote about experiments because raising, disciplining and educating children does require an openness to experiment and a desire to learn from each experience.

B. Adult reality checks with children

> The person who can most accurately describe reality without laying blame will emerge the leader.
>
> —Edwin Friedman

In 1962 the State of California opened a new institution for the treatment of delinquent adolescent girls near Ventura, California. The girls in the program were IC teenagers who had been in trouble with the law often. The uniqueness of the program was that the "treatment plan" for these girls was based upon a new type of therapy termed "reality therapy" under the direction of Dr. William Glasser. In this section of the book I will broadly discuss Dr. Glasser's Reality Therapy because I believe it has had a remarkable success rate with IC children that is as noteworthy today as it was fifty years ago. If it seems odd that I would be discussing a "therapy" in a book that has not been written for professionals, please do not give up on this chapter. It is my contention that the principles of Reality Therapy can be used by all of us despite our limited training. After all, the difference between guidance and therapy in many cases is only "intensity" (Glasser 1965).

You may recall that in earlier chapters I used William Glasser's (1965) words to define responsible behavior as behavior that allows a person to meet his needs without interfering with the ability of others to meet their needs. Thus, it is accurate to say that his major focus working with IC teenagers in Ventura was to help them fulfill their needs in a socially appropriate manner. When his students did things that interfered with the rights of others, Dr. Glasser helped them to do a reality check about their behavior. He would lead this gentle confrontation only after a trusting relationship had been established between himself and the student he was working with. I would imagine some of his questions may have included:

1. When you acted this way, what need were you fulfilling?
2. How do you think your actions affected others?
3. Did this behavior work for you?
4. What could you do differently next time to meet your need without getting into trouble with others?

Take notice that Dr. Glasser accepted no excuses, never mentioned a disability or diagnosis and spent very little time discussing a student's past unless it was directly related to the behavior event. He wanted students to take responsibility for the reality of their present behavior and the need to change this behavior in the future. Such a simple theory but so powerful in practice!

As an example of reality therapy in a school setting, I have described below an incident that occurred many times in my office and, I might say, occurs in many principal offices across the country on a daily basis:

> Edwin was brought to my office for hitting another student at recess. The conversation unfolded in this manner:
>
> PRINCIPAL: Edwin, why are you in my office?
> EDWIN: I hit James because he called me lazy.
> PRINCIPAL: I'll bet you were pretty angry.
> EDWIN: I am angry—it's his fault!
> PRINCIPAL: Edwin, you know school rules prohibit fighting. You will be suspended for three days, and we will need to have a meeting with your dad. Can you imagine what our playground would be like if everyone who was called a name slugged the other person?

EDWIN: There would be a lot of fights, and no one would feel safe.

PRINCIPAL: You are going home for three days, and you will miss the field trip to the river. James will probably have a consequence for calling you a name but will not miss the field trip. Are these the results you wanted?

EDWIN: No.

PRINCIPAL: Let's explore what you could do differently next time to take care of your anger without getting into trouble.

I am sure there was more to this conversation than is printed in this book; nevertheless, I hope you get the point of this story. The principal simply wanted Edwin to judge the realities of his own behavior before he developed a plan to change this behavior. In this context, the principal was being a leader by helping a child examine his own behavior without passing judgment.

Any discussion of Dr. Glasser's work at the Ventura girls' school would be incomplete if other important elements of the program were not discussed. The girls were enrolled in a high school program with academic and vocational classes taught together. In all cases the girls were handed more responsibility as they became ready for it and they were exposed to rich vocational opportunities. Dr. Glasser and his staff were as determined to help the girls find their strengths as human beings as they were determined to help the girls develop the ability to "reality check" their behavior. If a wayward girl who continually landed in jail for stealing could discover that she is better hairdresser than a crook, a new world has opened up to her.

Susan Scott (2002) once said, "There is something within us that responds deeply to people who level with us." In my experiences working with IC teenagers at Bishop Manogue Catholic High School I truly saw this version of "reality checking" in action. One of our staff members, Jami Hunt, could always be counted on to "level" with students to a greater degree than the rest of us. It was not uncommon to hear Jami say to a student in remote corner of the room, "And is this working for you?" Who would the students go to when they were in the most serious trouble? You are correct, it was usually Jami. The value of adults doing reality checks with children and especially teenagers was affirmed over and over on a daily basis in our program. Jami, Tony, and Nate continue to this day to have a profound effect on the students they serve because of their willingness to do reality checks with students in a manner that will *help students to do their own reality checks one day.*

Chapter summary

There are many children in our schools and in our homes who are not thriving well in their settings. Our challenge as adults is to not give up on these children and to bring them the resources they need to believe in themselves and to find their *voice* in life. Most important, we must see these children as "Intensive Care" (IC) children because there is an urgency to provide them the help they need right now. Continual disappointment and failure can have a crushing effect upon the will of these IC children to succeed in life.

There are no easy pathways to help IC children who are struggling to be successful in their environments. The parents and teachers trying to help these children must establish a pattern of purposeful behavior based upon three important principles:

1. These adults must look "inside themselves" to make sure their beliefs and behaviors are in the best interests of the IC children they work with. Attitudes of optimism, faith, patience and an appreciation of the "spirit" of all children can help inspire and influence IC children to improve their lives.
2. These same adults must examine their relationship with each IC child to make sure it is positive and built upon good listening skills, trust and a sense of caring.
3. It is important for all adults to do their best to help each child explore his or her strengths and give these children

the opportunity to use these strengths on a regular basis. A focus upon *abilities*, not *disabilities*, is the first step in helping IC children find their *voice* in life.

Strategies to help IC children improve their lives, unlike the principles they must be based upon, can change depending upon their effectiveness. For children displaying behavior problems, there is no doubt that reasonable and flexible rules at home and in school must be developed, taught and enforced consistently. Adults who succeed in helping IC children often infuse an element of choice in rule-making and consequence development. Lastly, meaningful and timely two-way discussions of behavior need to occur with adults providing nonjudgmental reality checks along the way.

The quest to help IC children be successful in life is a *spiritual crusade*. There is nothing more satisfying in life to see a child excel against all odds. We all have heroes who have achieved this feat because of an iron-clad spirit and, usually, a parent, mentor or teacher who has provided the encouragement, support and love to help these children remove the IC from their names, find their *voice* and leave a legacy for others to follow.

As a fitting conclusion to this book, I would like to briefly mention the stories of two individuals who have touched the lives of many people in profound ways and have completed the journey from being IC children to becoming inspirational role-models for generations to come. Neither one of these individuals presented major behavior problems in school; instead, they were individuals with special needs who benefitted from the timely help of caring adults in their lives. I tell these stories as a reminder to myself that *every child, no matter what his or her circumstances are, has the potential to be a beautiful wild flower.*

Anneli Crawford (1941–2016)

By the time Anneli was ten, she had endured more loss and sacrifice than most of us could ever imagine in a lifetime. Her father, a German soldier, had disappeared in the war and her mother had died in the Russian Occupation camp they lived in in Eastern Germany. With food scarce and temperatures cold, it was no wonder that Anneli and her sister would be susceptible to Scarlet Fever and near death as they struggled to endure the day-to-day misery of their encampment with their fifteen-year-old brother, Martin. Both girls survived their disease but had significant hearing loss the rest of their lives.

The three siblings were quite surprised one day when they were placed in a crowded cattle car on a train heading to Western Europe. Martin, acting as the girls' parent, took care of the girls during the long trip feeding them warm water with acorns in it and whatever bread he could find. Eventually, the three children arrived in Europe, boarded a ship to New York and later arrived in the home of Emil and Hattie Mittman, their new adoptive parents.

Was Anneli an IC child at age ten? I think so. Any child bearing the loss of her parents and the uncertainty of survival in an Occupation camp would need love, patience and consistency to recover from her ordeal. She received these gifts from her new adoptive parents and a lot more.

As time passed, Anneli became a school counselor and moved to Strathmore, California where she met her husband, Jerry Crawford. Together, Jerry and Anneli raised two wonderful sons, Duke and Eric, and they have been blessed with four spirited grandchildren.

Anneli Crawford retired from the Strathmore Union High School District after thirty-one years of service to the students and families of this small community in the Central Valley of California. She was a teacher, coach, counselor, continuation principal and superintendent during those years. The library of the high school is now named after Anneli Crawford.

There is no question that the experiences Anneli had as a child influenced her voice as an adult. She was a passionate believer in the freedom of individuals to have choices. Seldom did she have a conversation with her boys or students without inserting a statement about the choices they had in front of them. This belief in the freedom to make choices was probably the reason she was so successful with IC students in her role as continuation principal because these students, above all, needed to be treated with the respect and empowerment that having choices creates.

Just as Anneli's passion for freedom was an outcome of her experiences as a child, her incredible ability to listen intently to others was a special quality influenced by her loss of hearing. Throughout her life Anneli had to give 100 percent of her attention to listen to others because of her lip reading and struggles to hear the other person. Instead of shying away from conversations, Anneli became a remarkable listener to others who was empathetic and, at the same time, skilled at posing "reality checks" when called for.

Anneli Crawford was an amazing woman whose life story and contributions to her family, friends and educational community will never be forgotten. The extra care she received as a young IC child helped her to become a highly respected adult.

David Drakulich (1985–2008)

In the fall of 1992 I was asked to evaluate a second grader at Silver Lake Elementary School named David Drakulich. David was struggling to put his words on paper and concentrate in his second grade classroom. On that particular day I was in such a hurry to observe David in his classroom that I forgot to ask the teacher beforehand which student he was. After five minutes in the classroom, I knew the student I was present to observe. One student's desk looked like a wind gale had hit it and the student, who was well behaved, was drawing with a pencil crouched over his desk stockpile while the teacher taught grammar—it was David for sure.

When I asked David to come with me after twenty minutes, he gladly came and went to a small office to begin our assessment process. School psychologists normally talk to students for about ten to fifteen minutes to establish rapport and begin to understand the child's perspective on the world. After thirty minutes of discussion I reluctantly had to stop our talk because I did need to assess another student that day. I was so impressed with David's reasoning, verbal skills and imagination that I could have talked with him all day. When I looked at his writing, I could not understand a thing, but

David clearly explained what he had written in detail. I knew that David was an IC child who was gifted, challenged and possessed some very unique attributes as a person.

David's matriculation through school was not an easy journey. David and his parents had many meetings with school staff to find the best way to educate David. Teachers who appreciated his spirit and talents did well with David, but some teachers struggled to understand David. One theme that was present in each educational experience David had was his penchant for drawing and sketching in class. David's parents, Joe and Tina, recognized David's need to express himself in art and eventually hired an art instructor to help him develop his artistic talents. David developed an extensive portfolio of artwork that is on display today.

David Drakulich was sixteen when 9/11 occurred. Like many other students his age, David was profoundly affected by this event and ultimately joined the army in January 2004. David served in Afghanistan as a fire support specialist as a member of the Eighty-Second Airborne Unit. He was killed by an IED on an Afghanistan mountainside on January 9, 2008, while on a forward operating mission. David had parachuted during the dark of night and walked for hours to a point where he could relay information to international units preparing an assault on an enemy position. David's experience with sketching had helped him to draw the landscapes that enemy forces used for cover.

At his funeral, attended by several dignitaries including the Governor, David was heralded as an American Hero who had received the Bronze Star, Purple Heart and Army Good Conduct Award for his service to his country. David's NCO had this to say about David, "Sergeant Drakulich was a truly loyal, dedicated, hard-working trooper, who always seemed to humor us in every situation."

David Drakulich was an IC child who became a wildflower in so many ways. His parents helped him find his voice in his art and, "He learned to embrace himself as a very special and unique person." David's legacy is preserved through the David J. Drakulich Art Foundation: For Freedom of Expression. This foundation empowers and showcases the wellness of veterans (www.arthealswarwounds. com).

Bibliography

Amstutz, Lorraine Stutzman, and Judy H. Mullet. *Restorative Discipline for Schools: Teaching Responsibility, Creating Caring Climates*. Korea: Korea Anabaptist Press, 2011.

Amstutz, Lorraine Stutzman, and Judy H. Mullet. *The Little Book of Restorative Discipline for Schools: Teaching Responsibility, Creating Caring Climates*. Good Books, 2015.

Anderson, Richard C. *Becoming a Nation of Readers: The Report of the Commission on Reading*. Distributed by ERIC Clearinghouse, 1985.

Bates, and Ritchie. "Enduring Links from Childhood Mathematics and Reading Achievement to Adult Socio-Economic Status." May 2, 2013.

Biehler, Robert F., and Jack Snowman. *Psychology Applied to Teaching*. Houghton Mifflin, 1990.

Boynton, Mark, and Christine Boynton. *The Educators Guide to Preventing and Solving Discipline Problems*. Alexandria, Virginia: Association for Supervision and Curriculum Development, 2005.

Bronfenbrenner, Urie. *The Ecology of Human Development: Experiments by Nature and Design*. Cambridge, MA: Harvard University Press, 1979.

Buckingham, Marcus, and D. O. Clifton. *Now, Discover Your Strengths*. Pocket Books, 2005.

Chansky, Tamar Ellsas. *Freeing Your Child from Negative Thinking: Powerful, Practical Strategies to Build a Lifetime of Resilience, Flexibility and Happiness*. Da Capo Lifelong, 2009.

Chicago Manual of Style Sixteenth Edition (full note), formatting by CitationMachine.net.

Coloroso, Barbara. *Kids Are worth It! Giving Your Child the Gift of Inner Discipline*. New York: Quill, 2005.

Connellan, Thomas K. *Bringing out the Best in Others! Three Keys for Business Leaders, Educators, Coaches, and Parents*. Austin, TX: Bard Press, 2008.

Connolly, Theresa. *The Well-managed Classroom: Promoting Student Success through Social Skill Instruction*. Boys Town Press, 1995.

Covey, Stephen R. *7 Habits of Highly Effective People*. Simon and Schuster, 1989.

Covey, Stephen R. *The 7 Habits of Highly Effective People: Personal Workbook*. London: Simon and Schuster, 2005.

Covey, Stephen R. *The Eighth Habit Personal Workbook*. New York: Free Press, 2006.

Dobson, James C. *Dare to Discipline*. Vereeniging: Christian Art, 1989.

Dobson, James C., and James C. Dobson. *The New Strong-Willed Child*. Wheaton, IL: Tyndale Momentum, an Imprint of Tyndale House Publishers, 2014.

Dobson, James C. *The New Dare to Discipline: Answers to Your Toughest Parenting Questions*. United States: Tyndale Momentum, 2014.

Dreikurs, Rudolf, Pearl Cassel, and David Kehoe. *Discipline without Tears*. New York: Penguin, 1991.

Dunlap, Glen. *Prevent-teach-reinforce: The School-based Model of Individualized Positive Behavior Support*. Paul H. Brookes Publishing, 2018.

Durlak, Joseph. "The Impact of Enhancing Students' Social and Emotional Learning." *Child Development*, February 3, 2011.

Erikson, E. *Childhood and Society*. Norton, 1963.

Fay, Jim, and Charles Fay. *Teaching with Love and Logic: Taking Control of the Classroom*. Golden, CO: Love and Logic Institute, 1995.

Fountas, Irene C., and Gay Su Pinnell. *Guided Reading: Good First Teaching for All Children*. Heinemann, 1996.

Gibran, Kahlil, and Rupi Kaur. *The Prophet*. 1932.

Ginott, Haim G. *Between Parent and Child: New Solutions to Old Problems*. London: Pan Books, 1978.

Ginott, Haim G. *Teacher and Child: A Book for Parents and Teachers*. Collier, 1993.

Glasser, William. *Reality Therapy: A New Approach to Psychiatry*. Harper and Row, 1965.

Glasser, William. "The Quality School." *NASSP Bulletin* 75, no. 537 (1991): 132-34. doi:10.1177/019263659107553724.

Glenn, H. Stephen., and Jane Nelsen. *Raising Self-reliant Children in a Self-Indulgent World: Seven Building Blocks for Developing Capable Young People*. New York: Three Rivers Press, 2000.

Goleman, Daniel. "The Emotional Intelligence of Leaders." *Leader to Leader* 1998, no. 10 (1998): 20-26. doi:10.1002/ltl.40619981008.

Goleman, Daniel. *Working with Emotional Intelligence*. New York: Bantam Books, 2006.

Gorn, Susan. *What Do I Do When: The Answer Book on Special Education Law*. LRP Publications, 1999.

Gottman, John Mordechai., Joan DeClaire, and Daniel Goleman. *The Heart of Parenting: How to Raise an Emotionally Intelligent Child*. London: Bloomsbury, 1997.

Greene, Ross W. *The Explosive Child: A New Approach for Understanding and Parenting Easily Frustrated, Chronically Inflexible Children*. New York: HarperCollinsPublishers, 2014.

Irene Fountas, and Gay Su Pinnell. *Guided Reading: Good First Teaching for All Children*. Heinemann, 1996.

Hart, Sura, and Victoria Kindle Hodson. *The Compassionate Classroom: Relationship Based Teaching and Learning*. Encinitas: PuddleDancer, 2004.

Hensley, Michele, and Walter Powell. *The Well-managed Classroom: Strategies to Create a Productive and Cooperative Social Climate in Your Learning Community*. Boys Town NE: Boys Town Press, 2007.

Hensley, Michele, and Walter Powell. *The Well-managed Classroom: Strategies to Create a Productive and Cooperative Social Climate in Your Learning Community*. Boys Town NE: Boys Town Press, 2007.

Heward, William L. *Exceptional Children: An Introduction to Special Education*. Pearson Education, 2000.

Hunter, Madeline C. *Discipline That Develops Self-discipline*. Corwin Press, 1990.

Jones, Fredric H. *Positive Classroom Discipline*. New York: McGraw-Hill, 1987.

Kohn, Alfie. *Unconditional Parenting: Moving from Rewards and Punishments to Love and Reason*. New York: Atria Books, 2006.

Lahey, Jessica. "Poor Kids and the Word Gap." *The Atlantic*, October 16, 2014.

Levine, Mel. *A Mind at a Time*. Brain Books, 2004.

Lyubomirsky, Sonja. *The How of Happiness: A Practical Guide to Getting the Life You Want*. Piatkus, 2013.

Marshall, Marvin. *Discipline without Stress, Punishments, or Rewards: How Teachers and Parents Promote Responsibility and Learning*. Los Alamitos, CA: Piper Press, 2012.

Maslow, Abraham H., and Robert Frager. *Motivation and Personality*. Pearson Education, 1987.

Medina, John. *Brain Rules: 12 Principles for Surviving and Thriving at Work, Home and School*. Seattle: Pear Press, 2014.

Mendler, Allen N. *What Do I Do When...? How to Achieve Discipline with Dignity in the Classroom*. Moorabbin, Vic.: Hawker Brownlow Education, 2012.

Montessori, Maria. *The Discovery of the Child*. Ballantine Books, 1967. Translated by M. Joseph Costelloe

Mosak, Harold H. *Alfred Adler: His Influence on Psychology Today*. Noyes Press, 1973.

Nelsen, Jane, and Lynn Lott. *Positive Discipline in the Classroom: A Step-by-Step Approach to Bring Positive Discipline to the Classroom and to Help Teachers of All Grade Levels Implement Classroom Meetings: Activities for Teachers and Students*. Orem, UT: Empowering People, 1997.

Orszulak, Ed. *The Redemption Approach: 5 Timeless Principles for Re-engaging Tough Kids in School.* Chapin, SC: YouthLight, 2007.

Phelan, Thomas W. *Surviving Your Adolescents: How to Manage and Let Go of Your 13–18-Year-Olds.* Place of Publication Not Identified: Parentmagic, Incorporated, 2012.

Phelan, Thomas W. *1-2-3 Magic.* ParentMagic, 2014.

Piaget, Jean. *The Psychology of the Child.* Basic Books, 1972.

Popkin, Michael. *Taming the Spirited Child: Strategies for Parenting Challenging Children without Breaking Their Spirits.* New York: Fireside, 2007.

Pransky, Jack, and H. Stephen. Glenn. *Parenting from the Heart: A Guide to the Essence of Parenting from the Inside Out.* CCB Publishing, 2012.

Sagor, Richard. *Local Control and Accountability: How to Get It, Keep It, and Improve School Performance.* Corwin Press, 1996.

Scott, Susan. *Fierce Conversations: Achieving Success at Work and in Life--one Conversation at a Time.* New York: Viking, 2002.

Seligman, Martin. *Authentic Happiness.* Nicholas Brealey Pub, 2017.

Shore, Rima. *Rethinking the Brain: New Insights into Early Development.* Families and Work Institute, 2003.

Siegel, Daniel J., and Mary Hartzell. *Parenting from the inside Out: How a Deeper Self-understanding Can Help You Raise Children Who Thrive.* Brunswick, Vic.: Scribe Publications, 2014.

Stiepock, Lisa. *Tough Love: Eighteen Top Experts Share Proven Strategies for Raising Confident, Kind, Resilient Kids.* Simon and Schuster, 2016.

Stroufe, Alan. *Conceptualizing the Role of Early Experience: Lessons from the Minnesota Longitudinal Study.* 2010.

Tough Love, edited by Lisa Stiepock, 2016.

Tough, Paul. *Helping Children Succeed: What Works and Why.* Boston: Houghton Mifflin Harcourt, 2016.

Trelease, Jim. *The Read-aloud Handbook.* Penguin Books, 2013.

Walfish, Fran. *Why Empathy Matters and How to Raise Kids Who Will Be Empathic Adults.* Simon and Schuster, 2016.

Walsh, David Allen., and Erin Walsh. *Why Do They Act That Way? A Survival Guide to the Adolescent Brain, for You and Your Teen.* New York: Atria Paperback, 2014.

Wielkiewicz, Richard M. *Behavior Management in the Schools: Principles and Procedures.* Boston, MA: Allyn and Bacon, 1995.

Wong, Harry K., and Rosemary Tripi. Wong. *The First Days of School.* Sunnyvale, CA: Harry K. Wong Publications, 1991.

York, David, Phyllis York, and Ted Wachtel. *Tough Love.* Bantam Books, 1982.

About the Author

D oug Whitener has been a parent and an educator for forty-five years. He has served children in California, Alaska, and Nevada in many different roles, including, teacher, coach, guidance counselor, school psychologist, principal, special-education and student-support-services director, board member, university instructor, and consultant.

Mr. Whitener has presented at state and national conferences, contributed to a Federal training guide for ADHD students, participated in an International Roundtable on Special Education at Oxford University, and was honored to be recognized as the Washoe County administrator of the year in 2003. He has been a Danforth principal and is a trained PALS mentor for school principals. Mr. Whitener presently serves on the board for the High Desert Montessori School in Reno, Nevada, after completing two terms on the Parents Encouraging Parents (PEP) Board for the State of Nevada.

7/19/2019

Dear Meggin,

It is one thing to be an inspiration for teacher leaders; it is another thing to inspire people <u>one on one</u> ... you do this so well!

<u>Thanks</u> for your words of encouragement, advice, referrals and review

I hope their are some worthwhile ideas in this book for all of us to consider

CPSIA information can be obtained
at www.ICGtesting.com
Printed in the USA
FSHW011256160719
60072FS

9 781684 562886